NTC

NTC

A Primer of Modern Land Combat

Hans Halberstadt

Presidio Press ★ Novato, California

THE PRESIDIO POWER SERIES
LANDPOWER # 3004

For my stepson, SP4 Christopher Quentin Johnston, Scout Platoon,
Headquarters & Headquarters Company, 1st Battalion of the 61st Infantry,
and all the rest who have made the trip and fought the fight.

And for his mother, April, and all the mothers who love their soldiers.

Published by Presidio Press
31 Pamaron Way, Novato CA 94949

Library of Congress Cataloging-in-Publication Data

Halberstadt, Hans.
NTC: a primer of modern land combat/Hans
Halberstadt.
    p. cm.—(The Presidio power series. Landpower; #3004)
  ISBN 0-89141-313-8:
  1. Tank warfare. 2. Military maneuvers—California—Fort Irwin.
3. United States. Dept. of the Army. National Training Center.
I. Title. II. Series.
UG446.5.H26 1989
358′.18—dc19   88-30074
                                                                                    CIP

All photographs copyright © Hans Halberstadt, with the exception of page 123 and 134.

Half-title page: Sergeant First Class Jarrett of the 32d Guards holds a rocket-propelled grenade antitank weapon in front of a Soviet ZSU-23-4 antiaircraft system.

Title page: A VISMOD BMP overwatches the battle in the Valley of Death.

Printed by Singapore National Printers Ltd, Coordinated by Palace Press

Contents

Acknowledgments

As usual, the Army has been generous with its cooperation and assistance on yet another Power volume. My thanks to the staff at the National Training Center, particularly Captain Dutton and Staff Sergeant Carasco, who baby-sat me for two weeks. Then there were the wonderful 32d Guards, particularly Lieutenant Colonel Mac-Donald, Lieutenant Colonel ("Bad to the Bone") Monza, and Captain ("Mad Dog") Bernhagen.

Sixth Army Public Affairs came through with all sorts of help: Capt. Tom MacKenzie has once again told me all about the profession of armor; General Cole and Colonel O'Brien both shared insights on armor in general and NTC in particular. General Cole was one of the first commanders of the installation and was the source of much of the information about the evolution of the concept of armor.

Several members of the 3d Armored Cavalry Regiment from Fort Hood also did much to help, and foremost among them was Regimental Command Sergeant Major Ramsey.

I had also better thank both my wife, April, and my business partner, Vera Williams, for ganging up on me and helping with a complicated and sometimes confusing story. As with every Power book I've worked on, April and Vera asked the right questions at the right times, and I'm grateful once again.

There are a lot of others, and I'd like to recognize them all individually, but instead I will salute them as a formation. Thanks to all.

Glossary

AAR   After-action review.

APC   Armored personnel carrier.

BATTALION   Usually three companies with a headquarters, commanded by a lieutenant colonel. A tactical unit, the fundamental unit employed at NTC and throughout the Army.

BATTERY, COMPANY, and TROOP   Names given the basic unit of maneuver in the Army, usually about 120 people. Troop is a company in a cavalry organization. Battery is the term for the same basic unit of artillery and air defense artillery, while Company is used to define a unit of "leg" infantry, normal armor units, and most combat support and all combat service support.

BMP   Soviet light armor vehicle with big gun and antiarmor missile.

BRIGADE   Usually two or more battalions functioning as part of a division.

CALL FOR FIRE   Request for artillery supporting fires.

COMBINED ARMS TEAM   Organization of infantry, tanks, artillery, attack helicopters, and air defense units. Can be supported by Air Force and Navy tactical air.

CRUNCHIE   Tanker's name for infantry (from the noise produced when you drive your track over one).

CVC   Combat vehicle crewman helmet.

DRAGON   Man-portable antiarmor guided missile.

E TOOL   Entrenching tool.

FIST   Fire-support team, the people attached to a unit from an artillery battery who call for fire.

HOFFMAN CHARGE   Large blank charges that simulate the firing of the main gun on a tank.

LAW   Light antitank weapon.

LD   Line of departure.

M1   Current state-of-the-art main battle tank of the United States, featuring special composite armor, computers, and a gas turbine engine. Each costs about $2 million (or about a tenth the cost of a fighter aircraft).

M60   Former main battle tank, currently available in profusion, and upgraded with almost all the features of the M1, except the armor and engine.

MILES   Multiple integrated laser engagement system, a device used on a wide variety of weapons to provide some idea of who is doing what to whom without bloodshed.

Sergeant Burke, commander of the 3d Armored Cavalry Regiment's M1A1 tank Fox 22. His CVC and body armor have MILES sensors attached.

MRE Meal, ready-to-eat, the basic combat meal, also referred to as meal, rejected-by-everyone.

MRR Motorized rifle regiment, a basic Soviet maneuver organization.

O/C Observer/controller.

OP Observation post.

OPFOR Opposing force.

REGIMENT (1) Soviet: Normally two or more battalions functioning as part of a division. (2) American cavalry: three or four squadrons plus aviation, but not part of a division.

SABOT Expression for a high-velocity kinetic-energy projectile that relies on mass and inertia to punch through tank armor. The sabot itself is actually a device that falls off the projectile after it leaves the gun.

SAGGER Soviet antiarmor guided missile.

SOP Standard operating procedures.

SQUADRON Old expression referring to four troops (i.e., company-sized organization) of horse cavalry. In modern usage it *usually* refers to three recon troops—an HQ troop, a tank company, and a battery of self-propelled howitzers—but organization varies from division to regiment.

T-72 Soviet medium tank of recent design, many thousands of which are fielded by Bloc nations.

T-80 More recent Soviet tank that may incorporate many of the technological advantages of NATO vehicles, including thermal imaging, ballistics computer, and navigation computer systems.

TANK Heavily armored, tracked, fighting vehicle with large-caliber main gun and often several smaller machine guns. It is differentiated from other tracked fighting vehicles by

A 3d ACR tank squirms and scurries under the massed guns of the enemy.

two essential criteria—heavy armor and a large gun. Lots of tracked vehicles zip around the battlefield spouting smoke and flame, but the tank is the baddest boy on the block.

TASK FORCE (TF) Temporary organization of units assigned to one lieutenant colonel commander tasked with a particular mission. When a combat battalion level organization receives assets from another kind of combat battalion, a tank battalion gets an infantry company and becomes a task force.

TOC Tactical operations center.

TOW Tube-launched, optically tracked, wire command link guided missile; a vehicle-mounted, antiarmor weapon.

VISMOD Visual modification.

VULCAN Multibarreled gun with variable high rate of fire; mounted on an M113 and used for both air and ground targets. System includes a radar that is capable of seeing both target and bullet stream and matching the trajectories of both.

Warning Order

MAD DOG AND THE ATTACK ON PEANUT

At 0540 on a clear morning just before dawn, the commander they call Mad Dog climbed up on the T-72 tank he would shortly ride into battle. Taking his last opportunity, he dug out his can of Copenhagen snuff (the favorite brand of the tankers of his unit), extracted a healthy pinch, and inserted it neatly into a corner of his mouth, where he could enjoy it while he fought and annihilated yet another American armored unit.

The 32d Guards Motorized Rifle Regiment has the reputation for being the best of its kind in the world. So it was reasonable for Mad Dog and his crew and the other people in the "Soviet" tank company to feel a quiet confidence as the minutes ticked off toward the appointed hour of 0600, when the lead element of the regiment was to cross the line of departure. As the stars faded with the approach of daylight, the forms of the other T-72s, BMPs, and numerous other vehicles of the regiment began to materialize, and they were everywhere. At exactly 0550 the tranquility of the desert was broken by the sounds of every engine starting. Within minutes the air was filled with dust and noise as the tanks and personnel carriers moved up to their positions from which the assault was to begin.

Somewhere, miles across the desert, the American 3d Armored Cavalry Regiment waited with its amazing M1A1 Abrams main battle tank. The American enemy had helicopters for scouting and attack, they had Dragon and TOW antitank missiles, they had infantry and engineers. They had thermal sights far better than the ones available on the T-72. The Americans were expecting the attack and had prepared for days and nights. They had set mine fields and ditches and wire. Artillery fireboxes had been selected and the tubes were waiting for the call for fire. They had chosen their defensive positions with care, using the terrain to force an attacker into kill zones, where the American weapons would intersect in a focus of death and destruction.

Mad Dog and the other Soviet commanders knew all this. They had fought the Americans many times before. They knew what the weapons, terrain, obstacles, and people could and could not do—having learned the hard way. They knew this enemy regiment was inexperienced in combat, and that often in battle a cool head and a sound decision can defeat superior weapons and numbers. They also knew about where the enemy was, where his kill zones were, how he was trying to use the terrain, and where his obstacles were and where they could get around them. That information came from the scouts who had been infiltrated days before and had been observing and reporting everything the Americans did. It also came from the Americans themselves, who chattered away on the radio about all sorts of details of their defense.

Although the American weapons were glorious in their technological perfection, the Soviet equipment was not only good, it was available in large amounts. The Soviet plan was based on the idea that a huge, fast-moving force could overwhelm an enemy with speed, shock, and numbers. There were going to be losses, but that was expected and planned for. Victory should

A VISMOD T-72 fires a Hoffman charge, simulating the weapon "signature" of the main gun. The MILES for the main gun will not work without the noise of the charge.

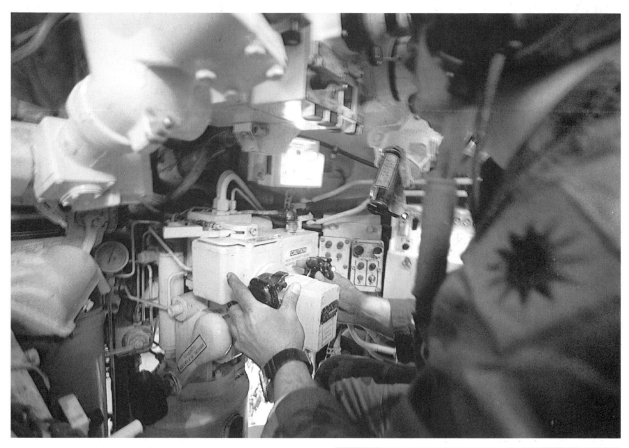

go to the survivor, and the Soviet commander simply had more raw material and experience to work with. The confidence of the 32d Guards was, therefore, pretty well founded.

The attack began with the regiment in column, the elements moving out together, gathering speed, staying as close to each other as the dust kicked up by the tracks would allow. For the first five kilometers or so, the tanks stayed on a dirt road, but as they started closing with the first known defensive positions, the elements began to deploy across the desert, Mad Dog and

Surrounded by the tools of his trade, a tank gunner searches the battlefield for targets. The control handles permit him to elevate and traverse the gun, operate laser rangefinder, provide lead for moving targets, and fire the main gun.

his company moving to the right and blasting along the rolling surface of the desert beside the lead element, sliding up his force to form a wall of steel and fire.

If you have ever seen an armored assault by a regiment or a brigade (few have, and fewer have survived), it is an experience never to be

A mixed bag of VISMOD combat power: a squadron hides in a wadi, preparing for tomorrow's battle. The OPFOR are masters of cover and concealment, knowing where every little refuge is.

forgotten. The tremendous speed, bulk, noise, and dust are overwhelming. A tank parked on display in front of your local National Guard armory looks graceless and awkward. It looks as though it might waddle around slowly, like some immense beetle. But in fact a tank is a fast, agile, graceful creature; when aroused and when in the company of its kind, it seems irresistible, and often is. Its main gun can kill other tanks two miles away, using a projectile that travels a mile a second. The gun sights are stabilized and computer controlled to permit accurate gunnery while moving at high speed. When these creatures are massed for either attack or defense, they are a force to be reckoned with, for there

are very few really effective ways of defeating an armored force that knows its business—except by others of its type. Armored combat of the kind called force on force is tremendously abrasive, rapid, and (frequently) decisive of larger issues.

As the regiment formed up and prepared to force its way through the first opposition, combat was joined. Off through the dust the flashes of the main guns of the attackers could be seen, and farther away the flashes of the guns of the defenders. Then there was a bang, clearly audible even over the noise of the tank. In the rocks that channeled the attackers, Dragon missile gunners emerged to launch their weapons, sometimes hitting, sometimes missing, and were themselves engaged by machine guns.

A battlefield is a complicated, abrasive place. Things happen in a dreamlike fog of dust and smoke, fear and exhilaration, noise and adrenaline. Individual events build on each other in subtle and dramatic ways, and there are always surprises. Quickly, the attacking force began to be eroded by the defenders, and dead tanks began to clutter the battlefield, adding themselves to the obstacles constructed by the enemy engineers. Mad Dog and his element had to slow down, which made them better targets, and soon the element was lighter by one, then two tanks. But at the same time that the defenders were killing the 32d Guards tanks, they were being killed themselves, being overwhelmed by force of numbers, and the pressure on the attackers declined. Just as the Mad Dog element prepared to break out of the kill zone, an American Cobra attack helicopter appeared from its hiding place in the

A Cobra prepares to strike: an AH-1 from the 3d ACR's combat aviation brigade ''unmasks'' to shoot a TOW missile at the Red Horde. It was killed seconds after this shot was made.

rocks. It fired a TOW missile, killing yet another of the tanks from the element. Then the Cobra itself was engaged and also died.

Mad Dog pressed on, and was quickly out onto the open desert. Behind his tank were the remains of the regiment mixed with the remains of the American defenders, littering the desert with destroyed equipment. A search to the left and the right revealed a few survivors, and those tanks and BMPs quickly formed on the leader, Mad Dog. To the front was wide-open desert and, ten kilometers across the valley, the objective of the attack—a hill mass called the Peanut. There was not a single American tank visible between them and the objective, though surely some waited in the wadis and ravines on Peanut.

Without a defender to slow them, the remains of the 32d Guards blasted across the surface, using speed as another kind of armor. There was still an enemy to defeat. They raced across the valley, Mad Dog thinking it was time to recharge his Copenhagen. In minutes the remaining force arrived on the other side, kicking up a few M1s from their hiding places, losing a few more tanks in the process, but destroying the defense. Using a small hill for cover and sneaking around the back door, the force was shortly on the Peanut and cleaning out the remnants of the defenders. Another Cobra appeared, then slithered away without being engaged. More M1s were discovered and killed, their expensive carcasses providing ineffective obstacles for the few remaining T-72s now swarming across the objective.

A VISMOD T-72 pauses momentarily in the fog of war. Dust reduces the normal visibility from miles to meters and the risk of collision is very real.

All dressed up with no place to go, Captain "Mad Dog" Bernhagen watches the survivors of his company drive on past his tank, now just one more bloated carcass on the battlefield.

Mad Dog killed one of the last defenders with three shots from the main gun, then worked his tank around a dead enemy and down into a small ravine facing the valley. In this quiet and protected spot he decided to reload both the main gun ammunition storage (now almost empty) and the Copenhagen (almost depleted, too). He and the driver climbed up on the turret and started the reloading process. It seemed like a satisfying victory.

But, it isn't over till it's over, and in this case there was at least one M1 left. The American chose this most vulnerable of moments to appear over the crest of the ravine. A yell from one of the crew jerked Mad Dog's head up in time to see the 120mm main gun traverse the few degrees needed to bear on the T-72, and in spite of the protected location, the victor became the vanquished and died a hero. "GOD DAMN IT!" the corpse declared with vigor, spitting over the

The dreaded Red Air makes its appearance at the edge of the fight, adding just one more element of hazard for the visiting team.

side of the tank. "Fellas, I'm really sorry, that was totally my fault. Y'all done real good. Boy, I really screwed up!" The crew was forgiving and matter-of-fact about their deaths. "Oh, that's okay, sir. We whipped their ass. You want a cold Coke?"

THE NATIONAL TRAUMA CENTER

This battle actually occurred, and in it the Soviet regiment prevailed, although at high cost. The tanks and the people in them fought hard, and learned how expensive war can be. The bullets they fired were laser beams. The deaths they inflicted and suffered themselves were electronic—temporary and physically painless. No funeral pyres and mangled steel, no shredded bodies and roasted flesh. Egos and imaginations, however, were often wounded. When a vehicle died on this battlefield, its gun stopped working, a yellow strobe light flashed, and everybody knew what had happened.

The battlefield is a huge desert landscape very much like that found in the Middle East. But it is also a classroom, and the lessons taught are ones of survival and success rather than death and defeat. The place is called Fort Irwin, California, a thousand-square-mile section of the high Mojave Desert in a remote area north of Los Angeles. It is the National Training Center (NTC), where armored units from throughout the United States Army come to train themselves to fight and win against the real Soviet and Warsaw Pact regiments they expect to confront if and when push comes to shove.

NTC is also known as the National Trauma Center, because it is an extremely stressful experience for the units that come to visit. The NTC takes normal American armor and mechanized infantry and puts them in a pressure cooker that comes as close to combat as you can get without bloodshed. It is designed to stress these units until they crack, and when they do crack, the failure is documented by a space-age instrumentation system. The failure becomes a lesson that (if studied and repaired) makes the unit much stronger.

Soldiers used to train for war by going to the field and playing a large version of "bang bang, you're dead!" Field exercises were opportunities for commanders to maneuver their elements against other elements, and see how their people dealt with road marches and getting along in the mud. But the training wasn't anything like war. In real war you are stressed in ways the U.S. Army doesn't permit in training. In war, the best lessons are taught by the enemy, and there is nothing like the snap, crackle, and pop of little chunks of metal around your head to make you pay attention to what you are doing.

There just aren't many combat soldiers left in the United States Army, men who've been taught their lessons under real fire. Since very few of today's soldiers have fought from a tank, some of the lessons of armored combat are being forgotten, unless, of course, we want to start training with live ammunition and living, breathing human targets who get to shoot back! The idea of NTC is to get as close to that as possible, without the bloodshed.

So NTC is designed to be a place where American units can visit just as they might some foreign battlefield. The idea is that they come here just as they would to fight for real. They bring with

Inside the "Star Wars" building the progress of the battle is monitored and supervised by everybody except Howard Cosell. The tension level here is extreme—but at least the air conditioning works. It's 105 degrees outside.

them the equipment and experience and people they would if the balloon went up, in the same frame of mind. At NTC, there is an enemy, not just evaluators. There are emotions and fears involved in going to NTC. It is not a camping trip.

The NTC is an interesting change in the way the Army thinks about training, and a tremendous improvement over the old kind. The old idea was to look good in the field, to hide weaknesses rather than reveal them. At NTC, the idea is to find those weaknesses and take a good look at them. At NTC everybody fails somewhere, somehow, and in failing they are supposed to become stronger and more successful. This is a radical idea for a peacetime army.

A visiting unit seldom beats the fabled 32d Guards, the resident OPFOR (opposing force), particularly in the early battles of a rotation. If they did they would learn little or nothing that would improve their odds in real combat. So the odds are always stacked against the visitors. Just the same, the battles are taken very seriously, and winning is always the proper objective. Emotions and careers are often involved. Officers have been relieved for poor performance at NTC, just as they might be on a real battlefield.

The National Training Center is a new kind of facility, offering a new kind of training. Its conception and execution have properly brought the Army great credit for innovation and imagination. In the few years it has been in operation, about a quarter of a million soldiers have attended its unique classes. There is no other training like this available in any army of the world.

But, as is often the case with new ideas, there have been criticisms of NTC, from within and outside the Army. It was expensive to build and is expensive to operate. It is hard on the vehicles and other equipment. It is stressful on the people who visit and on staff personnel. The units that visit are forced to endure a series of indignities, the chief of which is to get whipped by a bunch of rowdy lunatics wearing uniforms like Warsaw Pact soldiers, including a black beret with a bright red star on it. The visitors are not used to losing, and don't like the idea at all. There is resentment by the younger troops, who come hoping to beat the OPFOR. They will sometimes attack the OPFOR physically, leaping from one tank to another in frustrated rage.

When the NTC first opened in late 1981, a procession of network television crews and magazine reporters showed up to do investigative stories. They expected to write about how bad the Army was; after all, none of the units that came

T-72s rush through the Brown-Deadman Pass. The battle is half an hour old, and the tank in the foreground is already disabled.

13

to visit ever seemed to beat the "Communists." The reporters who came to blow the whistle on NTC drove away with a new attitude about the Army and the way the Army prepares to do its business. They came looking for failure and instead saw a tremendous success. They too became believers, and the word has spread. Officers and officials from many nations come to visit NTC; it is the envy of every army, probably including the Soviets'. Even the Israelis, who tend to train against a real opposing force, are delighted, envious, and amazed.

A sergeant major watches the battle. The tank on his beret identifies him as a member of an armor unit. The black beret and red star don't copy actual Soviet uniforms but suggest them.

At its foundation, NTC does two basic things for the units that visit. The first is called force-on-force training. The troops engage a real enemy on a battlefield like one they might actually have to fight on. They live, maneuver, and fight as complete battalions and brigades, far from the resources and routines of home. If the supply system doesn't work right, people go hungry for a while or run out of ammunition or fuel. They don't forget what went wrong, what should have gone right, and who was responsible. People concentrate on the business of an armored force, twenty-four hours a day for weeks at a time. This is a place to let the leaders lead and the followers follow, and success or failure is measured for all to see.

The other kind of training at NTC—live fire—is equally important but even more unusual. Live fire means loading up all the weapons on all the tanks and fighting vehicles and moving out to attack the enemy. When the enemy is sighted, he is engaged with real ammunition. The enemy during live fire is a computer-driven array of pop-up targets, and when they fire back, it is not with real ammunition but with Hoffman charges (huge blanks that simulate the flash and bang of the real gun). Still, it is closer to war than anyone in any other army gets in peacetime. Other units and other armies have live-fire exercises, but with all sorts of constraints and restrictions. The NTC lets people go out as maneuver units and blast away. The risk is that one tank will—in the heat of the moment—shoot another, or do something else that isn't completely safe. It happens. People make mistakes, sometimes bad ones. Well, combat isn't completely safe, nor is training for war.

Why do we need tanks and infantry in this age of missiles and nuclear weapons? With all the money spent on technology, tanks and infantry seem outdated and rather indecisive. But that is not the case. Even in the very recent past—as in the Arab-Israeli wars—tanks have proven to be decisive in conflicts.

The idea behind tanks and infantry, in fact the idea behind the whole Army, is that the control of ground is the foundation of conflict resolution. And no one can win the Land Battle but the guy on the ground with the gun. Everybody else on the army team helps the infantryman, the common foot soldier. And the tank works with and for infantry. Tank tactics are essentially the tactics of the infantry—fire and maneuver, bounding overwatch, movement to contact, and the rest.

Since WW II there has been a lot of tension in Europe, a classic standoff. Western politicians and planners are convinced that there is a sufficient threat of Soviet imperialism that it is prudent to prepare a defense against an attack. The Warsaw Pact nations keep in the field facing the West an amazing force of armor and infantry. It is quite capable of blasting across Europe at the rate of 100 kilometers a day. The force outnumbers us about four to one, and there are few illusions about what would happen in an invasion. So, the Army must contemplate how it could fight and win the large land battle if conflict should begin in Europe. How do we fight a war with these guys and win?

The machines and the men at the National Training Center are rehearsing for a performance that some of them may have to attend sometime in the future, sometime in their career. Soldiers and historians know that wars come along with unfortunate regularity in the affairs of societies. Armies exist as conflict-resolution devices, to provide a credible deterrence in the hope that conflicts might be discouraged and, if not resolved by peaceful means, then resolved quickly and at low cost in our national interest. That is why we have tanks, soldiers, and the National Training Center.

The Quest for Realistic Training

Back in the mid-1970s a series of unrelated developments evolved that made NTC possible. One was a concept of more realistic training for combat that began during World War II and reached maturity during and after the war in Viet Nam. During the 70s there had been experiments with a cadre of professional OPFOR soldiers who toured the Army teaching the doctrine of the anticipated enemy to the troops who were to play the role of the aggressors in war games. This program was called Red Thrust and was based at Fort Hood, Texas. Red Thrust began with two battalions out in the Texas desert, and within a short period of time the students knew more about the business than the teachers. Why? Because they were practicing the techniques every day out on the training battlefields. This rapid proficiency was noticed.

At about the same time several new technologies were being developed that had implications for the Army, and officers with imagination and vision took notice. Very early in the evolution of the laser, someone came up with the idea of using the device to simulate a weapon firing. Other people were considering the use of computers to record training events as they developed.

Then somebody noticed that Fort Irwin was not only vacant, but had room for large numbers of people to pound on each other without upsetting the neighbors. Fort Irwin has wide-open spaces, mountains, and desert; it looks like the sort of place you'd find the Israelis fighting the Syrians.

A heavily customized Huey with a strange paint job masquerades as a Soviet Hind. The real Hind is a formidable attack helicopter and a real danger to armor.

Fort Irwin is about a thousand square miles of desert, but it is *interesting* desert. There are high mountains, broad valleys, little hills, and wadis. There are broad, open spaces for maneuvering, and plenty of cozy little spots to hide outposts or battalions of defenders. There is virtually no one who will be annoyed by a little gunfire in the night. There is no danger of a loose artillery round hitting any civilian. It is isolated in almost every respect, and is one of the most remote garrisons in the Army. The town of Barstow, the closest real settlement, is about thirty-five miles away. The main post area with its PX and administrative buildings is a small enclave of offices, warehouses, facilities, and housing typical of any army installation, but it looks as though it was deposited on the desert by an alien hand. This is not a friendly landscape, but it's as friendly as it gets; here is where the vehicles are stored and maintained, where the water and food and fuel come from, where the only real link with home—the Burger King—is located.

The mountains and valleys impose on the landscape certain limitations. There are three major maneuver areas, each separated from the others by a major mountain range. Two are used for force-on-force engagements, and the third is normally used for live-fire activities. Each is between six and twelve kilometers (four to seven miles) in width and twenty-eight to forty-five kilometers (seventeen to twenty-seven miles) in depth.

A vision evolved of a place where large units could slug it out with a real enemy under conditions that were not only realistic, but also were documented in detail. This documentation was the key, because it meant that the students could see an almost instant replay of their efforts, and they could really learn in a way nobody had ever learned before—short of bloodshed. It was a radical vision.

During the 70s and early 80s, it all came together. The multiple integrated laser engagement system (MILES), a weapon scoring technology, was invented and the Army bought the kits by the tens of thousands for rifles, tanks, machine guns, and rockets. Microwave sensors and transmitters that were suitable for the task were designed and built. Designers and officers huddled over maps and conference tables, plotting and scheming how best to wire Fort Irwin's thousand square miles with sensors and relays and all the other technologies that would be required to document a realistic fight by brigades and regiments of tanks and infantry.

The Army surrendered hundreds of excellent and experienced officers and sent them to Fort Irwin as observer/controllers (O/Cs) to teach and to learn. Their job was to watch carefully as the units and individuals performed, and afterwards give a critique in the after-action review (AAR). These observer/controllers were the foundation of the human part of NTC. They were joined in the field by several hundred OPFOR soldiers. The O/Cs and the OPFOR were asked to do what no other large units did—spend most of each year in the field, most of each year away from their families. Saturdays, Sundays, and holidays were workdays for everybody at NTC—just like war.

When the first soldiers started showing up at Fort Irwin, the program was far from a smooth operation. They found barracks leftover from WW II, with sand inches deep on the floor. The commissary didn't even have refrigerators that worked. The tanks and other equipment were unreliable and there weren't enough of them.

Near the Whale Gap, a company commander and his platoon leaders conspire about defensive positions for tomorrow's fight.

The Army had decided, for the first time, to run the installation by civilian contract, freeing soldiers to train instead of maintain and administer. It was, at first, a disaster. The contractor thought the job could be done with ninety people, fifteen of whom were tracked-vehicle mechanics. The situation really called for hundreds. There were supposed to be two complete sets of vehicles for the visitors to use—one set to be in the field with a rotation, the other set in the shop being fixed from the previous war. It didn't happen; they got about a set and a quarter.

Nobody knew anything about Fort Irwin, so there were lots of snafus. People back in Washington looked at a map and saw many lakes on the thousand square miles of the installation. So the new recreation center began receiving shipments of boats for the troops to use in their leisure

19

Sergeant Gordon Tom, gunner on Fox 22, studies the battle-field as the enemy forces attack toward his position.

hours. They got sailboats, rowboats, windsurfing boards, inflatable boats, and boats for fishing and waterskiing. The ''lakes'' at Fort Irwin, however, are desert lakes and almost never have any water in them. Fort Irwin is one of the driest places in the nation.

There were other problems and miscalculations, and it took years of effort and sacrifice to put the whole thing together. Creating the new post was like inventing an art form—with a committee. Contracts were written and rewritten. Equipment was designed and built and installed, then it didn't work. Relay stations were constructed on the barren peaks of many mountains around the battlefields. Cameras and transmitters were bought and tested. But the complex technologies were not always reliable. A special five-ton van was built with video playback of microwaved signals of the after-action reviews. It didn't work, so the first rotations had their AARs sitting in the sand rather than in the special van. But they learned something anyway, and the technicians finally fixed the van.

There was a lot of improvising. How, for example, do you suggest to a tanker that he is shooting at a T-72 when there are very few of the Soviet tanks for sale on the open market? What you do is design a kit of fiberglass panels that can be bolted on a similar vehicle. So the Army started making VISMOD (visual modification) kits right at Fort Irwin, and putting them on M551s, which were available for the asking.

Although there were problems with the first few rotations, the bottom line was extremely encouraging. There were certainly lots of elements of the training plan that were not yet working, but they were rapidly being fixed. And despite the problems, the kind of ''discovery learning''

that the designers had hoped for was working wonderfully. The learning curves for both the home team and the visitors were steep and up all the way. Within a year or so, by about mid-1982, the rotations were running fairly smoothly, with all the technological and tactical concepts in place and functioning as planned.

MILES

Until quite recently, there was no accurate, effective way of scoring battles between units short of using live ammunition and then having people shoot at each other. For a variety of reasons, this approach is normally reserved for formal occasions, and for carefully selected opposing units. But when the laser was invented, with its bulletlike beam of light, it quickly suggested to several army officers the idea of a combat training scoring system. The MILES system was invented and perfected for this purpose, and is now used extensively throughout the military, not just at NTC.

The MILES is now used by many nations around the world as a tactical engagement scoring system. It is based on an eye-safe gallium arsinide laser transmitter, which can be coded to represent various weapons systems, from rifles to tank guns. These little transmitters are clamped to the barrels of all sorts of weapons, and when a blank round is fired, the noise triggers the transmitter, which sends its pulse downrange, right where the bullet should go.

The MILES transmitter and receiver on a Cobra from the 3d ACR's combat helicopter brigade. MILES is used on all direct fire weapons, from rifles to missiles.

There are receptors on just about everything that moves on Fort Irwin, and the receptors are as ingenious as the transmitters. Not only will they tell you if you're being near-missed or hit, they can tell what is doing the shooting, and whether or not you deserve—in the current tactical situation—to die. So a soldier can shoot at a tank with his rifle, and will have no effect. But if he shoots at a tank commander standing in his hatch, he can kill him if he's in range— and if he's a good shot. The vehicles all carry small black boxes that display the kind of weapon shooting and killing, so tank crews in particular know who got them. The soldiers all wear harnesses with receptors on them that also bring the sad tidings of miss, near miss, hit, and kill.

Weapons like the Dragon or TOW missile, which have a long flight time, must be operated much like the real weapon, and you have to track your target for seven seconds to score a kill with the MILES-equipped missile systems. The detector on the tank senses a hit or a near miss; if near miss, the strobe flashes twice and the crew hears two beeps on the intercom. A hit (but not a kill) produces four to six flashes and beeps. A kill results in a continuous flashing and tone and, if the target is suitably equipped, a cloud of smoke. The main gun and the machine guns stop working, and the crew is supposed to shut down the tank, gun tube pointed at the ground. The vehicles all have small radio transmitters that tell when they are shooting and when they are being shot at, as well as the kind of gun or missile that is firing or hitting. All these data are sent by radio and microwave back to the big computer, which somehow sorts it all out and displays the information on several kinds of screens, each showing different data.

A lot of fiberglass and an old M551 Sheridan make a VISMOD BMP, complete with plastic Sagger missile. The real BMP is smaller, sleeker, and more difficult to acquire.

This is a complete data recording system for every shot fired, every radio transmission, every movement of every tank and unit on the ground. It includes television images from manned and unmanned cameras. Everything is time-tagged and stored on a huge computer. Every mountain peak has a microwave relay transmitter. Mobile television vans record the action. Laser beams substitute for bullets. When a tank fires its main gun or machine guns, a transmitter not only sends the information to the computers back in the Star Wars building, it also provides information about where the tank was when it fired, and whom it fired on.

THE 32D GUARDS

The computers and the MILES systems and the dramatic landscape of Fort Irwin are impressive training aids, and mark NTC as a special

The helmets are Soviet issue, and so is the vehicle the driver operates—a MT-LB in excellent condition. Their crews like them, but spare parts are tough to find.

A BRDM scout car in the OPFOR motor pool is parked next to its brothers-in-arms, far from home. There is a lot of Soviet armor to study at NTC, and some of it runs.

Business end of a VISMOD BMP. A belt of MILES sensors surrounds the turret. The "kill" light is to the commander's right, the Hoffman charges and data transmitter antenna to the gunner's left.

place. But the stroke of genius, the thing that has really gotten the attention of the military world, was the invention of a Soviet-style motorized rifle regiment, complete with vehicles and weapons and numbers. It is built from two normal American battalions, one armor and the other mech infantry, and is augmented by visiting infantry and engineer units from all over the Army. The soldiers who augment the OPFOR attend an OPFOR academy, where they are trained in Soviet tactics, weapons, uniforms, and doctrine. They consider themselves part of this elite unit and are a formidable opponent for the visitors.

There is even a large collection of real Soviet tanks, trucks, and engineering equipment, as well as armored personnel carriers (APCs) and recon tracks, mortars, and artillery pieces that are avail-

able for anyone to inspect. There are T-55 and T-62 tanks, a BMP, an MT-LB, and BRDM—all Soviet combat vehicles. Some have holes in them, and nobody in authority will tell you where the tanks came from. If you have to think about fighting the real thing, it's nice to know what they look like up close; most have a VISMOD vehicle alongside to show how they're simulated on the battlefields. Up close, you see things that are a little surprising: The quality of the equipment is better than the Soviets often get credit for. These are not the crude, coarse, antiquated machines you see described in newspapers. Some of the designs do look like they might belong in museums, but the tanks have a sleek, domed turret that looks like it would shrug off almost any kind of projectile. The Soviets obviously know how to make a good tank.

The real Soviet vehicles are mostly not running and are too few and precious to fight with. Consequently, the regiment uses American vehicles that have been visually modified to look like the real article. These VISMOD tanks, APCs, mobile guns, and antiaircraft weapons systems vary in their ability to convince, but some of them are good counterfeits. The modifications are the result of fiberglass kits that are bolted onto hulls and turrets. The workhorse of the 32d Guards is the BMP with its 73mm cannon and Sagger missile. During a regimental attack, more than ninety of these BMPs will swarm across the battlefield. One variant of the BMP is the ZSU, with the ability to shoot at both air and ground targets with its four-barreled 23mm cannons. Then there is the Soviet-style artillery piece, the 123mm self-propelled howitzer.

One of the real Soviet vehicles on the battlefield is the MT-LB, which the Soviets use as a multipurpose vehicle; at NTC it is used primarily as a troop carrier. The NTC has a dozen or so MT-LBs in running condition, and they maneuver with the VISMODs. The crews wear real Soviet helmets, and think well of their mounts. But they won't tell you where the helmets came from, either. The real curiosity is a set of four brand-new, shiny green Warsaw Pact personnel carriers that are occasionally seen zipping around the parking lots of the main post area. Rumor is that they came from Yugoslavia. They are low, sleek, and exotic as hell.

Take that, you commie rat fink! An M1A1 cuts loose from a dug-in position on the live-fire range while an observer does his duty. The O/Cs spend more time in the field than just about anyone in the Army.

No real Soviet helicopters are available, so some are invented. The UH-1H model is also visually modified to simulate an enemy. It still looks like a Huey with a glandular problem. The paint scheme, though, is convincing, and the sight of that big red star over the battlefield is impressive. The helicopter is equipped with 53mm rockets, a 30mm chain gun, and an AT6 wire-guided missile system, all of which are plastic but MILES equipped, and so are capable of scoring kills.

The 32d Guards Motorized Rifle Regiment is actually two garden-variety armor battalions that have been tweaked and twisted into an organization that mimics the behavior of a Soviet unit. The designations of these battalions on the Army's roster of units are actually the 1st and 2d Battalions of the 61st Armor. In addition to the skills and activities that have made them famous, these two battalions are fully functional, normal American tank units with a full set of M60A3s and a regular set of wartime skills and assignments. Their unique role as the OPFOR has gotten them a lot of attention, some of which they could live without—or so they say.

The resources the 32d Guards have available are light ones, and in order to give the appearance of a full regiment, they have to cheat a little. The two battalion commanders trade off being the regimental commander and the regimental planning officer. These two men are aware of the spotlight that shines on them and their commands, and are concerned that their work be appreciated in the proper context.

The OPFOR commander says:

I have a normal U.S. Army tank battalion. It may be hard to believe, but underneath all this is a normal—to outward appearances ill disciplined—typical tank outfit that is basically crude in its endeavors and violent when it gets at those endeavors. We screw up things just like the BLUEFOR does. You name it, and we are just like they are. The difference is that the things we do—come to the field and train—we are allowed to do in an ideal way. Let's get in the field all the time!

For most commanders, NTC is a chance to come out here and try things. They have ideas about the way to fight their units, and this is a place to put it on the ground and see what happens. And if he's reasonably competent, if he knows his business, he'll learn a lot and get the job done. The guys it really shows up are the ones who've been off doing other things for a few years, who have not studied this business very much and have been doing other than infantry or armor jobs. They come out here and try to live off their superior intelligence and intellect, and it doesn't pay off when you have to figure out what an aiming stake is.

I enjoy the motivation that we put into our guys, and to see that motivation pay off in a successful mission. It is not my job to boot-stomp some guy into the ground. There is a spirit of winning, and a chance to get at that out here and to continually try things. How do you motivate this guy, as opposed to that guy? How do you come up with a plan that is going to win? And a lot of that comes from an attitude of "I gotta go after him." And it changes every time. Every time is different! I think that every one of them, when they leave here, are better than when they arrived. And that's the key.

There has been a lot of pressure to make NTC into a place where officers can show off and climb the promotion ladder. There was (and sometimes still is) a view that an NTC rotation is a test of a unit's war-fighting ability, and a lot of soldiers view the OPFOR as a real enemy. Visiting units sometimes become desperate to beat them, desperate enough to cheat. For example, once a patrol was hidden in the dumpster by the motor pool to report when the OPFOR moved out. Other soldiers were caught with shaved keys for the MILES systems, allowing unlimited ammunition for the weapons, while others covered the sensors on themselves or their vehicles. But NTC is really supposed to be an institution of higher military learning. The OPFOR are the best friends an American armor or mech infantry unit could ask for; they are here to teach fighters how to fight successfully, to win, and to live. It isn't war, it isn't a game, and nobody is supposed to win or lose. Despite pressure from people who want the place to be something else, NTC is a practical seminar in life, death, and combat power, taught in the most vivid way possible.

The commander of the 32d Guards, Lieutenant Colonel ''Bad-to-the-Bone'' Monza directs his forces as they obliterate yet another capitalist/imperialist/Yankee unit.

All About Armor

Since the National Training Center is an armor and mechanized training facility, the place is abundantly stocked with nearly every kind of combat vehicle used by the units that visit. There are long rows of M1 and M60 tanks, a growing horde of M2 and M3 Bradley fighting vehicles, parking lots full of M113 armored personnel carriers in every permutation, gaggles of M108 self-propelled howitzers, and many of the wheeled all-terrain vehicles called Hummers. There are also long rows of equivalent Soviet bloc tanks, personnel carriers, supporting artillery, and combat support vehicles.

Armored combat is a very complicated experience, and despite the impression of a casual observer, there are lots of players who are not using tanks at all. So you ask, what is a tank then? Armies use many kinds of armored and tracked vehicles, some with guns on them. The United States Army, for example, has the M551 Sheridan, currently in use only by the 82d Airborne Division. Despite the tracks, turret, and the 152mm gun, the Sheridan is not a tank but an armored reconnaissance vehicle, and with pretty light armor at that. A smart Sheridan commander will turn tail and run from a Soviet tank! The gun, turret, and armor are designed to protect a crew from artillery fragments and small arms fire. The M551 is light enough, in fact, to be air delivered by low-altitude parachute extraction (LAPES). You don't get to do that with an M1.

Then there are the boxy little armored personnel carriers that are available in huge numbers in any armored unit. Also, there is the huge

M88 tank recovery vehicle, which looks like a building with tracks. These are all armored vehicles, designed to fight the Land Battle alongside the tanks.

A tank in any army these days is a heavily armored, heavily gunned, highly mobile crew-served weapon. One of its most important components is its tracks. A tank moves, and moves quickly. It is irresistible except by others of its kind or by heroic measures. A tank is the one weapon that really scares the hell out of the infantry, the one weapon they really have a hard time defeating alone. A garden-variety tank today weighs about fifty tons, and has one big gun that shoots a projectile about five inches in diameter, several smaller guns, and a lot of electronics, usually including a computer. It can shoot accurately on the move, hitting things a mile or so away with devastating power. It sees in the dark, and many can see through smoke and fog. It has three or four people aboard. They are protected by armor that is built from layers of different substances and may be from an inch to a foot thick, depending on which part of the tank you are measuring. It costs a lot of money.

Tanks are offensive and defensive, and operate in groups of two to two hundred. They tend to be the leading edge of a task force of many combat skills and resources that function as a team, providing mutual support. Like the fighter aircraft overhead, tanks are dramatic technologies and expensive weapons systems that are part of a much bigger organism, the combined arms team.

Tanks operate in an environment alive with the instruments of death—mines that can blow the track off, or blow the tank apart; wire-guided missiles, fired by helicopters, other vehicles, and

---

On the road again! An M60A3 from Fort Benning's 197th Brigade jams off to another one-night stand. Although not as fast as the M1, the M60 is still fast enough.

even carried around by infantry for opportunities; helicopters and other platforms with hypervelocity rockets that propel steel rods to tremendous speeds, capable of punching through the toughest armor.

Tanks defend themselves in ways that are diverse, ingenious, and sometimes primitive. In the defense, given time and terrain, all tanks are dug in and sometimes provided with a roof. An enemy looking across a battlefield at a prepared defender will not see any tanks at all, only the eyes and combat vehicle crewman (CVC) helmets of the track commanders standing in the turret. But by driving forward thirty feet up a carefully designed slope, the tank is raised to reveal the gun tube and permit the turret to aim

and fire, after which the tank retreats back into its hole. Although it seems like a perfect defense, that doesn't exist in warfare: A dug-in tank is an attractive target for an enemy attack helicopter and a good target for artillery.

Another hazard for the dug-in tank commander is one most people would not think of—a rifleman with a simple, bolt-action rifle, usually in 7.62mm caliber. Actually, the rifleman would not be alone; he would be part of a team, a sniper team. The 7.62mm bullet will hardly scratch the paint on a tank. But a track commander can't really see very well from inside,

In a properly prepared position, a tank can safely hide until the moment it must reveal itself to fire.

and given a choice will almost always stand in the hatch. The visibility may be better, but the armor is useless. He will not see the bullet that kills him.

American sniper teams pride themselves on their ability to hide and shoot and kill under battlefield conditions. Snipers set up shop where enemy armor will attack. They will have a day or so to build their "hide," an almost invisible position where they will wait for the enemy forces to approach. They plan on killing tank commanders in the hatches of tanks moving a kilometer away, with single-shot kills to the head. One man shoots; the other spots the round. The spotter watches for the little vapor trail of the bullet going through the atmosphere and the red mist that fills the air from an accurate head shot. They start by killing the commander, then shooting off the track's antenna so the crew will be unable to spread the alarm. They will work their way down a column, one tank at a time, for as long as they can get away with the trick.

So for all the armor, and despite the big gun and the heavy machine guns (and the little ones, too), tanks are mortal. They can be beaten, and can die quickly, and in vast quantities. Tank battles tend to be messy. Burning hulks of machines, and of men, litter the terrain. The Israelis know how expensive tank battles can be; so do the Soviets and Germans who survived the Second World War, and so do the veterans of the breakout from Normandy who followed Patton across France. Armor is not a cheap game, or for the faint of heart.

An M60A3 moves forward in the gathering dusk; thermal sights and night vision devices permit US forces to emphasize night fighting.

37

HOW TO DRIVE AN M60A3 TANK

The basic American tank is now the M1, a very large, expensive, intricate, and effective weapons system. It is powered by a gas turbine engine, similar to the ones used on propjet airplanes, and when it moves the only sound is the squeak of the tracks and a quiet but powerful rush of exhaust. The beast can move at tremendous speeds—up to fifty miles an hour—across open country. It can shoot with great accuracy at that speed, day or night, through smoke, dust, rain, or fog, using thermal sights and a stabilized, computer-driven gun that fires a variety of ammunition, all of which is quite lethal. There are four men in the crew—a commander, a loader, a gunner, and a driver. They are, in effect, an infantry fire team with tremendous mobility, protection, and potential. The M1 is augmented by huge numbers of M60 tanks, which are a little less state of the art, and a lot less expensive. The M60s are being upgraded with the same gun and electronics used on the M1, and this improved version, the M60A3 model, will continue to be an essential part of the Land Battle for a long time to come.

Let's do something very few people are permitted to do—take a tour of a tank and try out its various stations and systems. Since so much of the M1 is still classified information, we'll tour and test an M60A3, which is old enough now to permit careful scrutiny of some of its basic systems but is still close to state of the art and a certified killing machine.

The first problem is to get aboard. There are several approved ways of boarding the beast, and the one you use will depend on your strength and energy. The young troopers hop gracefully aboard; the older officers and NCOs use the little toe hook on the front slope and haul themselves up. Once on the deck you scramble up on the turret, where you can look down into the depths of the tank through the commander's or the loader's hatch. The commander's is bigger; sit on the edge and swing your feet inside, then lower yourself first to the seat. Do not stuff your foot through the thermal sight (TTS); the cost of the TTS is about 20 percent of the value of the whole tank, which probably makes it the most expensive TV set anywhere. Be nice to it, though, because it can save your hide.

A quick scan reveals that there is very little room for people inside a main battle tank. The thing is crammed with elegant instruments and equipment. While the outside of the tank is as sleek as a seal, the inside is cluttered and complicated.

LOADER'S POSITION

In the left rear of the turret, next to the commander and close to the breech of the gun, sits the junior man on the team, the loader. If you are new to tanks and tank crews, this is where you begin to learn your trade. You sit facing the breech of the gun, and buttoned up you have a very boring view. You can't see out. Your business involves removing one round at a time for the main gun, placing it in the breech, and pushing it home with your fist. On the M60 the ready ammunition locker sits just astern of the breech. It holds the food for the big gun in front of you. Here are rows of gray aluminum cases in their neat racks, waiting to be called upon. There are different kinds of rounds, and it is your business as loader to instantly extract the one the commander asks for and feed it to the gun.

GUNNER'S POSITION

After you've been a loader for a while and have behaved yourself, provided coffee for the others on demand, and fed the gun with efficiency and dispatch, your leaders may let you try out for the gunner's seat. It is forward and below the commander's station, and to get there you have to worm your way over and around the gun, down into the little space in the forward part of the turret. To be useful as a gunner you need to master a set of controls that look like those on a fighter aircraft. The view is much more restricted in this position, but the intent is similar, and so is the nature of a lot of the controls. You have controls for the computer, the thermal sight, the laser range finder, and the gun itself. The first time you sit here it seems impossible that anyone could learn to manage it all, particularly in the heat of battle. After you've done it a few times, though, it starts to get easier. Why don't we try it out? Have a seat.

The MASTER POWER switch is already on, so you've got power for the sights and turret. We'll work through the checklist, each system in its proper order. Passive sight first; it's the backup. Set the brightness level for the reticule, check the elevating quadrant and gunner's periscope, open the ballistic covers, and adjust the headrest and filters. Check focus and you're good to go on the passive sight.

Now for the thermal sight: set to TEST (which prevents the laser from firing), MODE to STANDBY. The thermal receptor has to chill for fifteen minutes to work, but it's worth the

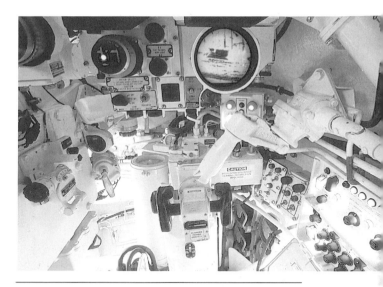

Gunner's station on an M60A3. That's an M113 armored personnel carrier under the crosshairs in the thermal sight, and he'd better behave. The crank is the emergency turret control; the two black grips below control the 120mm gun.

wait. Open the ballistic cover for the sight, and it's good to go, too. You have to share this sight with the commander, so make sure the switch on the panel is in GUNNER position, then take a peek and see what's out there. Adjust RANGE FOCUS and POLARITY, and set FIELD OF VIEW to NAR (narrow), and what have we got? Well, if it isn't a T-72! The thermal sight is a green and white image, and shows things in terms of hot and cold. The tank is warm, particularly the engine area, and shows up bright against a dark field; if you want, you can reverse the polarity, and hot will be dark. It's your call.

Now for the laser range finder. Set POWER to ON, adjust focus and reticle brightness, set MANUAL/RANGE FINDER to RANGE FINDER and LIGHT to TEST. They all light

A gunner engages the enemy in his sector as they swarm through the infamous Whale Gap. Despite the numerous controls and displays, the gunner has to act with trained instinct; he "plays" the main gun with the precision of a concert musician.

and the electronic displays show 8888, so the range finder is good to go, too. Next, run the self-test sequence on the computer, set air temperature and approximate altitude, and your systems are ready to shoot.

Hmm, that T-72 is still out there, and I think he sees us. Quick, MODE to ON, lay the reticule on the center of mass using the two handgrips that traverse the turret, and elevate the gun. Push RANGE button; the laser range finder indicates 1,200 meters, easily within range. Set ammunition select switch to APDS (armor-piercing discarding sabot), which is what we better use on this guy, before he uses the same on us.

Let's go back and load up with a sabot round (a small-diameter, high-velocity antitank projectile). Pull one out of the rack; breech switch depressed, and it opens; slip in the round and

42

get your hand out of the way, and it closes with a thunk.

Okay, the tank is still there in the reticule and the computer has worked out the solution to the gunnery problem, taking into account the wind speed, temperature, range, type of ammunition, and all the other factors. Make sure the vent blower is ON to get rid of the fumes, and set LASER RANGE FINDER to AUTO and STATIONARY/MOVING switch to MOVING. Now you've got to use the handgrip controls to track the target to set the lead and fire the laser. Depress and hold down the LEAD LOCK button under your right thumb. There is a trigger on both grips, and pulling either fires the gun.

There isn't much of a bang inside, but the recoil rocks the tank. Through the sight you can see the tracer fly downrange to impact the hull of the T-72. Nice shot. Consider yourself a hero.

COMMANDER'S POSITION

After you've been a gunner for a while and behaved yourself, probably reenlisted once and made sergeant E5, you might be tapped to be a tank commander (TC).

The commander is a sergeant or one of the company officers, and he has usually been around tanks long enough to know how to read a map while lurching over rough terrain, keeping an eye out for the enemy and an ear on the company radio net while he's working with his own crew. Tank commanders, in other words, are skilled jugglers. (The commanders of tank commanders are masters of the art.)

As commander, you live in the turret surrounded by radios and sights. You can sit or stand while the tank moves, but you prefer to stand—the visibility is better. If you're sitting

it is because the tank is buttoned up. If it is, you can still see pretty well through the thick glass prismatic viewing devices that ring your hatch.

A .50-caliber heavy machine gun is mounted where you can operate it, buttoned up or not. A sight and an aiming device are positioned pretty much in front of your nose, and the two will meet forcefully if the driver should abruptly stop the heavy metal monster! A rocker switch neatly fits your thumb, and with very little practice, you can track the cross hairs of the .50 caliber on a moving target half a mile away.

If the gun happens to have a belt of ammunition in it and the target is lightly armored—a Soviet BMP, for example—a squeeze of the red trigger on the front of the grip will produce a mild vibration in the tank. Little bright dots of red will dance into the field of view and begin to form a cloud around the target. Some will bounce off and fly into space at curious and rather beautiful angles. Dust will rise to obscure the vehicle. If your target happens to be within effective range (and you, of all people, should be able to tell) and at a vulnerable angle, the half-inch, three-ounce projectiles will pound the surface of the victim. Some will penetrate its armored hide. Some of these will strike crew; others will strike fuel and ammunition. Through the sight, though, all you see is the fireball when the fuel cells feel the heat from the incendiary rounds, and they touch off the ammunition stored nearby. The BMP's Sagger missile adds its fireworks to the show without endangering the Americans for whom it was designed.

When the target happens to be another tank, a variation on this sequence transpires. In a tactical situation, the whole crew is always searching for targets, always examining the environment. The first to see a target calls it out. Often it is the commander, from his vulnerable but excellent vantage point, who sees the enemy first. Tank combat happens fast, and seconds count. Crews practice the drill until it becomes a fluid and graceful performance.

DRIVER'S POSITION

We'll finish our tour of the tank by climbing out of the turret and scrambling forward to the driver's position under the gun tube. Hop in and adjust the seat.

As driver you sit forward, alone in your compartment. You have the best seat in the house. With the gun tube forward, though, you are closed off and protected from events inside the turret, where the rest of the crew work and live and die. You sit in a fully adjustable seat, which takes some adjusting. Two instrument panels face you at eye level; one is for the usual information any driver needs—speed, oil pressure, engine

Driver's-eye view in an M60: the narrow vision blocks may not offer much of a view, but they keep you a little safer. Those are the gas pedal and brake in the usual spots.

temperature, and the rest—and the other panel is full of warning indicators.

As with a car, there is a brake pedal. Instead of a wheel there is a set of handlebars. If you can steer a tricycle, you can steer a tank. On the grip is a switch for the intercom microphone. The driver, like the rest of the crew, wears a helmet specially designed for the needs of armor crewmen who call it a CVC. The Army calls it a helmet, combat vehicle crewman. It protects your skull from the inevitable impacts with the beast you inhabit, but it doesn't cover everything. Old tankers often show the effects of broken noses. The CVC has a microphone on the left side that perches on the end of a little wire boom. You can adjust it to a place right in front of your mouth where your commands and responses will best be picked up. The microphone won't stay where it is supposed to because of the tank's vibration, and you will have to adjust it frequently as you blunder across the landscape.

The M60 lets you drive buttoned up or unbuttoned. The first is good for protection when chunks of metal are flying around; the second is more comfortable in safe situations, and gives better visibility. This is different from the M1, which you have to drive buttoned up. Both the M60 and the M1 use a system of prisms and mirrors to give you a view of the outside world, 120 degrees to the front, and both have night-vision systems to keep you out of the ditch on those dark and stormy nights.

The job of driver is critically important in the heat of battle, where he becomes a microtactician. He must position the tank to the best advantage, often without guidance from the tank commander. This is particularly true when one or more of the crew have been killed or wounded.

The best seat in the house is right up front—until the metal starts to fly. Then you button up quickly. The driver is isolated from the rest of the crew in his little steel foxhole.

If you are going to drive, the TC has to be able to count on you. The fundamentals are rather easy for anyone who can drive a car, but there are some differences. First, set the MASTER POWER switch to ON, FUEL PUMPS to ON, and TRANSMISSION in N (neutral). Give it a little gas with the throttle and then press START. The engine fires quickly, and the oil pressure gauge shows a needle in the green. Adjust the rpms to 1,200 and lock the throttle to allow the engine to warm up.

While you are waiting for the engine to warm, look around at your office. You've got three periscopes for protected vision forward, and a thermal viewer for driving at night. There are lights for the tank, but you will seldom get to use them, and almost never in the field.

The crew of a 155mm self-propelled howitzer pose with a high explosive projectile. The 155 is heavy artillery that stays close behind the tanks and fires in support of them on the live fire engagements.

Okay, let's take it out for a little tour of the battlefield. Foot on the brake; shift from N to L (for LOW range), just like a car. Foot off the brake and on the accelerator, give it some gas, and off we go, tracks clanking and screeching. The steering control works as you'd expect, and soon we're rumbling across the ground at twenty miles per hour. The sensation is one of smoothness and control. The M60 is comfortable over moderate terrain and at moderate speeds. Shift to HIGH range and speed up, and we start to wallow a little, blasting across the desert at thirty miles per hour. Be careful of wadis and tank ditches! Okay, let's get this thing back before they notice we took it.

THE CREW

A tank crew is an extension of the tank commander, and he in turn is an extension of the commander of his platoon, company, battalion, regiment, and so on up through what the military calls the chain of command. The whole crew serves the commander's eye and his trigger finger. If the commander has done his job properly, his tank systems work reliably and his people do the same. He leads them as a unit, a team. When the crew and the commander go to work, few words are spoken. Few are needed if the training has been good.

The commander's first word to the crew is "GUNNER!" This is the warning order. With a single word the commander has told the crew that he has a target in sight, and is about to engage. With this single word, the commander also tells the crew that they may have been seen—that the other tank may be preparing to engage them, and that the first shot fired will probably be fatal. Who will fire first?

"SABOT!" is the second command, a heartbeat from the first. It is easier to say than hypervelocity armor-piercing discarding sabot, which is the right and proper name for this particular ammunition. The projectile is a simple piece of steel, a solid block of metal that weighs about 5.5 pounds. It flies through space at the rate of almost a mile a second, and when it hits, its kinetic energy will easily carry it through many inches of the most sophisticated armor, even the new Soviet reactive armor. The loader pulls an antiarmor round from the ready ammunition locker behind the gun and slides it into the chamber of the 120mm gun in one smooth, practiced move, shoving it into place. It takes a second. The breech closes on the round with a solid clunk.

"UP!" reports the loader. The gun is loaded and off safety, the crew clear of the recoil. The gun is ready to shoot. Two or three seconds have elapsed.

"TANK, FRONT!" is the third command, and it tells the gunner what he is supposed to kill. It is a T-72, far across the valley—3,000 meters through smoke and dust. It is invisible to the eye except through the thermal imaging sight, but there it is with the cross hairs glowing against it. The gunner doesn't think about how he does his work; it is totally instinctive. The sight is aligned on the target center of mass, far away toward the farther reaches of the gun and the system that aims it, but still within range. A push on the laser range finder switch fires a pulse of coherent energy that bounces off the T-72 and back in less than a heartbeat, providing accurate data on the distance to the target. Without any attention from the crew, a computer generates a solution to the ballistics problem, taking into account a dozen elements, then aiming the gun.

"IDENTIFIED!" yells the gunner, though he need not yell over the intercom. Although the tank and the gun are now blasting across the surface of the battlefield at forty miles per hour, the gun locks onto the precise angle that will deliver a small, very heavy steel dart on a killing trajectory into the enemy vehicle, which is at this very moment preparing to fire back.

"FIRE!"

"ON THE WAY!" responds the gunner, just as he fires. The whole process takes three or four seconds. The tank reacts to the recoil of the gun, but there is no real noise from the weapon inside the buttoned-up vehicle. Through the sights both the commander and the gunner watch the bright red tracer as it flies through space to impact low on the turret of the T-72, followed instantly by a flash and flame.

Tank combat is terribly quick, terribly dangerous, an excellent filter for the quick and the dead. A good crew can get off three shots in ten seconds. If the first shot doesn't do it, another follows almost instantly. Three laser-aimed, computer-adjusted shots, each of which stands a good chance of hitting, and if it hits, of killing. Russian tanks, American tanks, whatever, the first shot is likely to be the decisive one.

Preparation for Combat

If you're a tanker, sooner or later you and your unit will deploy to the battlefields of the National Training Center. The word will come down months in advance, and if you happen to be a commander of a battalion, or a commander of a single tank, the news will definitely elevate your blood pressure. It is going to be an ordeal, and it is not likely to be a lot of fun.

If you're like most tankers, you think you belong to an excellent unit, one of the best tank outfits in the United States. If you are equipped with the glorious M1A1 Abrams, you know you've got a wonderful weapons system. If your unit happens to have the Bradley as well, you know that you've got the potential for beating up the OPFOR because the Bradley is a BMP killer, big time. But that is just potential; that is all in the future. How well you do as an individual, as a unit, and as a team will remain to be seen under the harsh glare of the computers and the O/Cs.

The process begins about two months before the rotation with a visit from the NTC staff, a kind of warning order for the brigade commander, who is asked to define what he wants his unit to learn during the rotation, something called the Mission Essential Task List. Based on the list, the NTC staff designs a scenario for that particular unit. The scenario is based not only on what the commander wants to accomplish, but on the experience of the unit. If they have been to NTC before, they can be assured that the current rotation will be full of new fun and games.

Later, the unit is visited again. Ops group arrives to brief the troops and the leaders on what to expect and how to prepare. The unit works toward the date on the calendar as though it were a final exam. They begin to rehearse and inspect equipment and people. Some of them have been to NTC before, and they know what to expect. The junior officers and NCOs try to get the troops fired up to be ready to teach the OPFOR a few lessons, but everyone knows what the win-loss record looks like at NTC. As the weeks tick off and the appointed day looms larger on the calendar, the units continue to try to work out the kinks in a thousand different systems, a thousand different routines. They stay in the offices late and get to the motor pools early. There are extra inspections and extra trips out to the training areas. There is a saying in the Army: Train the way you expect to fight. The units train long and hard, in small groups and large.

A typical rotation schedule lasts twenty days, and begins with the arrival of a task force of an armor battalion and a mechanized infantry battalion, with a supporting "slice" of artillery, air, combat, and combat service support units— a total of about 2,500 soldiers who will operate about 750 vehicles. They bring their own aviation "assets," usually between seven and fifteen attack helicopters. They will be supported by the Air Force, which generally flies A-10 ground support attack aircraft for the Blues out of George Air Force Base, about seventy miles away.

At Fort Irwin the troops will set up camp, draw some of their equipment from pre-positioned stocks, and after two or three days move out. As in Europe, a large stock of equipment sits ready for war. There are three battalions worth of tanks sitting on the ground at NTC,

Three little APCs huddle under the nets—the tactical operations center for the 32d Guards on the eve of battle. This is the reliable source of fresh coffee and the latest info.

one each of M60A1s, M60A3s, and M1A1s. For six days the two battalions will fight together under their brigade commander. Then one will go off to the live-fire corridor for four days of blasting away, after which it will trade places with the other battalion.

At last the day arrives. The duffel bags are packed and weapons drawn. The wheeled vehicles and the aircraft have already left by train. An advance party has gone ahead to set things up. It's onto the airplane and off to sunny California.

Buses are waiting for the troops at Norton Air Force Base, and the men are transported the 100 miles to Fort Irwin. Just before they go through the main gate, off to the right the troops see a rock formation covered with the colors, insignias, and comments of past visiting units. It is called Painted Rocks, and leaving your unit's mark here is a tradition that goes back almost fifty years. Patton trained his tankers here before taking them to North Africa and beyond. There are the crests and mottos of the 5th Engineers, back in 1985, of 1st Platoon, 2d of the 16th—the Pathfinders, the 10th Mountain Infantry Division, the fabled 101st Airborne, the 197th Brigade; all left their mark, alongside that of medics, infantry units, aviation outfits, and even some Marines. "We came, we saw, we kicked their ass," it reads. The first two comments are certain, but the last is suspect. There will be a fresh coat of paint on one of these rocks in a couple of weeks, memorializing the visit of your unit.

Painted Rocks is just about the only mark the troops see on the desert, other than an occasional rusting hulk of an old target tank or truck. The landscape is big—tremendously so—and empty. There is a cleanness to it, somehow, even in the dust. It is a sterile kind of landscape, with very few hints of mankind. No trash blows in the wind; the troops clean up after themselves. There are no billboards or fast food concessions along the road, not even a house, although here and there a house trailer sits in strange isolation. The pleasures and distractions of what passes for civilization fall away behind the buses as they roll down the last hill into main post.

Finally the buses turn off into the barren ground they call the Dust Bowl; the doors open and it is time to dismount. Stepping off the bus, you see acres of sand and dirt only partially shaded by steel overhead covers, the most basic of shelters. At the margins of this tremendous space can be seen parked tracked vehicles, and wheeled ones too. Many of the regiments, companies, and battalions have already arrived and are setting up all the comforts of home. The comforts of home, in this case, are limited to shelter halves joined to make that classic of U.S. Army housing, the pup tent. They are erected in proper military rows, by the thousands. It is hot and dusty, and the glare is terrific. Welcome to the NTC.

Happily, the cooks have arrived early and set up operations, and a hot meal of real food is waiting. Enjoy it, because you are about to endure a few weeks of MREs and T rations. The MREs are the official rations of the American fighting man, and consist of freeze-dried and otherwise preserved food that the Army calls "meal, ready-to-eat," but the troops like to call "meal, rejected-by-everyone." Field soldiers know to bring hot sauce to add to almost everything (except the candy). Old field soldiers bring all the canned food and other commercial chow they can stash with their gear without getting caught.

When there is nothing else to argue about, the most popular topic of discussion is whether the MRE is or is not better than the C ration it replaced.

When you arrive at the Dust Bowl, you are effectively at war. The clock is ticking and there is a lot of work to be done. On Day One you get to meet your faithful (you hope) steed, and one by one the platoons go off to inspect and complain about the vehicles they are offered. The tracks at NTC get used hard and often, get

Painted Rocks, redecorated by visiting units since World War II with unit insignia and occasional fictions of imagined victories over the OPFOR.

more miles put on them faster than anyplace else in the Army. Some of them are tired; others are really shot. Wiring harnesses are frayed, and bearing seals leak. Some defects are expected and repairable; others are excessive and will prevent you from doing your mission. There are arguments about equipment, and negotiations between officers and contractors. An NTC rule:

Thou shalt not engage in pissing contests with the contractors. The units do the best they can, accept what they have to accept, and sign for their vehicles.

The rest of Day One and all of Day Two are spent working on the vehicles and the MILES systems, and generally getting ready for war. Occasionally the troops see strange-looking soldiers in black berets moving around the area—the fabled 32d Guards; well, hostilities haven't really broken out yet.

At night you will get a chance to rest, and rest is going to be very important in the days ahead. It doesn't take long to set up your shelter, roll out your sleeping pad and bag, and otherwise set up shop. The powers that be have decreed that guards will be posted on the MILES equipment, but they don't tell you why anyone would want to steal it. So, when it is your turn, you stand guard in the chill of the desert night.

While the troops stand guard and prepare the

Two BMPs and a T-72 blend into the twilight near the OPFOR TOC not far from the John Wayne Hills and Siberia.

A Bradley prepares to move out—Day Three, the Dust Bowl.

tracks, the S2 and S3 sections are hard at work with their own intellectual kind of guard mount and preparation for combat. In tents and in the back of command tracks, the staffs concentrate on the planning they have to do to fight and win the land battle that everyone knows will begin very, very soon. Commanders and the commanded plot and scheme far into the night. There is some intel information coming in already. There will be more. The first order comes down from regiment on the third day: Prepare to execute a movement to contact.

THE BASICS OF ARMORED COMBAT

Combat does not simply happen; it is planned and executed, by both attacker and defender, in a tremendously complex and well-orchestrated ritual. The Army refers to this process as command and control. If you happen to be a commander, you do not have to prepare to fight each battle from scratch, but rather from an intellectually and organizationally prepared position.

Let's take a look at the policies and procedures behind the planning decisions being made this night in the Dust Bowl.

The kind of forces that play at the NTC are armor and mechanized infantry units, working as task forces, usually of battalion size, but sometimes as full brigades and regiments. An armor unit is a pure tank and IFV (infantry fighting vehicle) team, with lots of firepower but vulnerable to enemy infantry. A mechanized infantry unit rides to work in armored taxis, usually the M113 personnel carrier or the Bradley (M2) fighting vehicles. Each of these units starts life as a purebred one thing or another, with its own set of virtues and vices, but neither unit goes to war alone. Instead, the armor and mech infantry units are blended to make teams and task forces.

First, there are some concepts called the *imperatives of combat*. The commander makes sure the power of the force is concentrated on the enemy through the techniques of fire and maneuver. He must understand the plan he gets from his commanders and use that guidance to form his own plan, rather than perform a solo act. He must communicate his plan with vivid clarity to his subordinates and motivate them to carry it out quickly, as ordered, with confidence in victory. The commander should use a flexible style of command that doesn't stifle subordinate leaders (and followers). He needs to have a way to get timely and accurate information, and he must use it to make timely and effective decisions.

PURPOSE OF OFFENSIVE OPERATIONS

Destroying the enemy's fighting force is the only sure way to win, so you undertake the offense to destroy enemy forces. There are related but secondary purposes for conducting an offensive operation, which include taking decisive terrain, to gain information, deceive or divert the enemy, deprive him of resources, or pin his forces in position.

FUNDAMENTALS OF THE OFFENSE

- SEE THE BATTLEFIELD: You have to understand the force that opposes you in depth and detail, and, when you are attacking him, understand the way he intends to defend. This includes his doctrine, and the number, size, type, location, and strength of the units that oppose you. You need to anticipate their capa-

An M1A1 hustles off to join its mates. The "bustle rack" on the back of the turret holds tools, a five-gallon water jug, clothes, MREs, and track links.

bilities and weaknesses. You have to understand the terrain you will fight on. You will need to be forward during the battle to see what is happening and to keep the momentum moving forward.

- USE YOUR WEAPONS TO BEST ADVANTAGE: In particular, the platoons of your command need to support each other.
- CONCENTRATE OVERWHELMING POWER ON ENEMY WEAKNESSES: If you can't find a weakness, create one through surprise, massed firepower, isolation of an area of his command, or concentrating your forces on a small area of his front.
- SHOCK, OVERWHELM, AND DESTROY THE ENEMY: When you develop a weakness in the opposing force, exploit it with all the mobility, firepower, and shock action you have available.
- PROVIDE CONTINUOUS MOBILE SUP-

PORT: The attack eats up fuel, ammunition, and vehicles. To keep things going a commander has to anticipate these needs and to provide for replacements.

These concepts are the foundation of American armored combat philosophy, and are known by heart by every armored and mechanized infantry officer. But until these officers come to the National Training Center, these concepts are likely to be abstract ideas rather than a way of doing business. NTC is where the ideas become reality.

TYPES OF OFFENSIVE OPERATIONS

There are three types of attacks at the company level—movement to contact, hasty attack, and

Defense in sector, live fire. Each of the flashes on the ground is an enemy tank firing. They've successfully pushed deep into the sector and are about to overwhelm the defense. Each flash comes from a computer-controlled pop-up target.

deliberate attack—and they all are tested at the NTC.

- MOVEMENT TO CONTACT: When you don't know exactly where the enemy is or what he is doing, and you still want to fight him, you conduct a movement to contact, after which a deliberate or hasty attack is made. Using the smallest possible force to make the initial contact (a section or a platoon), the force maneuvers toward the enemy using the terrain to best advantage and maximum security. Platoons support each other, and are ready to provide either fire or maneuver to help other platoons nearby. The technique of traveling overwatch (a movement technique that lets a force cover ground with some security) is used until contact seems imminent, and then bounding overwatch (slower movement with greater security) is used.

Security becomes essential and is obtained in several ways. One of these can be speed, which makes it harder for the enemy to react; the flip side is that you can all get killed quickly if you stumble into a well-prepared defense. Security is also improved when you can use cover and concealment, but if the enemy is smart, he knows where the cover and concealment are, and looks for you there. If you're smart, you use artillery to suppress defenders along your covered and concealed route. The artillery can shoot smoke or antipersonnel ammunition or mines, all of which will help distract the other team while you go looking for them. Artillery is a big part of armor ops.

You need to plan for contingencies. You've got to anticipate what can go wrong before it does, and to look for choke points, river cross-

ings, large open areas, and areas where you think the enemy might be. Then you should plan how you're going to deal with these areas. Often the scouts or the lead element get to be the heroes and cross the danger area while everybody sits and waits to see if they get blown away. If they don't, they set up security and guard the area while the rest of the force crosses.

When the first small arms fire starts pinging off the tank's hull, it is time to dismount and deploy the infantry forward of the armored force. This is the best security against Soviet-style defense in depth. Otherwise, you will start losing many vehicles to rocket-propelled grenades (RPGs), an antiarmor weapon.

The infantry must move out smartly and fix the enemy positions, then the armor can roll into the attack, preferably with organic 4.2-inch and 81mm mortars firing for indirect cover. The artillery batteries in the rear cannot generally provide the accuracy at "danger-close" (300 meters) ranges needed for good suppression, so the mortars ride along for these contingencies.

When your lead element bangs into the other side, there are four things they have to do, and they are supposed to do them in order (but really fast). The first is to return fire to engage and suppress the enemy. They immediately deploy as they return fire, heading for the nearest cover and concealment. If you've just been ambushed, the cover and concealment is likely to be far away, and on the other side of the loyal opposition. You then have the choice of assaulting into the ambush or making a run for it, if possible. While all this excitement is going on, you are expected

to let the rest of the team know what's happening by making a report. Usually, it is the commander or the XO who gets to call up battalion and scream into the mike. The fire-support team (FIST) is expected to call for fire, a request for artillery on the bad guys. It is the company commander's sacred duty to determine what to do next from a short list of choices. He can execute a hasty attack, he can bypass the enemy, or he can defend and call for help. Whatever he elects to do, he's got to call up battalion and tell them what

Engineers from the 7th Infantry Division support the OP-FOR. Here they rehearse the technique of breaching an obstacle, a dangerous task because machine guns and rifles normally protect against just such efforts.

he's up to. Whatever he decides, they probably won't like it.

- HASTY ATTACK: Doctrine says that once contact is made, the company or team will use the technique of fire and maneuver. The platoon that found the bad guys will become what is called a base of fire, which means that they sit tight and shoot at the enemy with all they've got. This serves the noble purpose of getting the enemy's attention while other platoons keep shooting until the maneuver element starts an assault on the enemy. The maneuver element blasts away at the objective as they move toward it, while at the same time the base of the fire platoon, the distant artillery, and any available mortars are all giving the place their undivided attention. The attack by a team involves tanks and infantry, and it is up to the commander to decide how far the soldiers get to ride before they are asked to bail out and get to work. The tanks and the infantry then attack together, supporting each other.

- DELIBERATE ATTACK: A deliberate attack is designed to break through a defense into the weak area behind the lines. A company team usually does this as part of a bigger force, and may get the nod to grab an important piece of real estate or to work around an enemy strong point to quickly break through the lines. The company has more time to prepare for such an attack, and consequently should have a lot more information to work with. This entitles you to a well-prepared plan, and should get you an actual recon and—in training—a rehearsal. You can expect the chance to mix and match forces and equipment suited to the job.

Although rehearsals are part of doctrine and training, armor combat veterans will tell you that even in the most relaxed environment, a combat unit will rarely have the luxury to rehearse a deliberate attack even if there is theoretically time to do so. That time will get used for maintenance, resupply, and getting some badly needed rest. It will be a rare moment on the modern battlefield when a maneuver battalion can stop for twenty-four hours.

ORGANIZATION

All armor leaders from the top of an organization down to the tank commanders are expected to have some basic qualities in order to complete their missions: a sense of awareness to events as they unfold (difficult under the stress of combat), an ability to react quickly and take advantage of a fleeting chance, and a willingness to take the initiative—to see what is wrong and fix it. But the fundamental quality expected from armor leaders is common sense, a defense against many of the hazards of the battlefield. This is tempered by an expectation of aggressiveness, a constant effort to complete the mission successfully, to win as a unit and to support the overall plan.

TIPS ON LEADERSHIP

Every leader at the National Training Center—and throughout the entire Army—should know his job, himself, and his soldiers. The soldier needs to be informed. He needs to see his leaders setting a good example. A leader must make sure tasks are clearly understood, supervised, and accomplished by a clearly identified individual or group. Soldiers should be trained as a team. They need sound and timely decisions from their leaders. A leader is supposed to seek responsibility for himself and develop it in his subordinates. He uses his unit within its capabilities, not taking on more than he can handle. He takes

---

The OPFOR leaders receive the order at the TOC. Briefings are long, detailed, and use a precise format.

A platoon leader and other officers carefully copy graphics onto their maps during a briefing. Careful note-taking is a required skill for armor officers since so much depends on careful coordination of hundreds of details.

the responsibility for his actions, individually and as a leader of a unit; his unit's failures are his failures.

PLANNING THE MISSION

All this is theory. It is the summary of the lessons learned from thousands of combats in hundreds of wars over the decades and the centuries. But it is not until a commander finds himself on a battlefield that it all begins to mean anything. At NTC these concepts come alive in ways that are deeply traumatic. That is the idea. Brigade, battalion, company, and platoon leaders have to perform regardless of weather, personal problems, missing or damaged equipment, lack of sleep, and the failures of others. Excuses will not count at NTC. The imperatives of combat and the other basics of the troop-leading procedure will be the basic game plan for the entire immense team, and they will have to be followed if a leader is going to help the team win.

There is a standard ritual for leading the troops, and it involves eight steps that are intended to turn you into a hero, or at least accomplish the mission. It begins when you receive from your battalion the mission that tells you that you've got a job to do. Then you study the mission while watching the clock. You are supposed to use a third of the time remaining to plan the mission and leave two thirds for your subordinate leaders to get ready to do the work. You put the subordinates on notice right away, however, with a warning order so they can make preliminary preparations. Then you make a tentative plan, using a format called METT-T, which requires you to consider the mission, enemy, terrain, troops available, and time available. Your plan will probably require the help of other units, so you have to coordinate with them from the outset. Will you need artillery? Helicopters? Special weapons or communications equipment? The chaplain to perform the last rites? Then you make some preparations for moving people as a unit, telling them who is going, where and when. You get ready to perform a reconnaissance, using the time remaining in an efficient manner. Finally, you decide when and where you're going to let the troops in on your masterful plan for winning the war.

The basis for the plan being developed this night is something called SOP (standard operating procedures), a basic script with which all the players are familiar. The SOP mandates that in a certain situation, you're supposed to do a certain thing. It helps everybody coordinate and anticipate events before they happen. When the battle occurs it is too late for the commanders to have any more than a broad-brush influence on the outcome. The SOP is the point of departure, the foundation for the way the unit fights. If it is a good SOP—and the unit is trained well— the unit becomes a kind of living, reactive organism that deals with threats and opportunities in an automatic way. It's called "playing from the same sheet of music."

An SOP is a set of instructions having the force of orders. Everybody knows what it is, which means that far fewer questions need to be asked or answered. An SOP is flexible. Commanders and staffs design their own, based on situation and preference and the SOP supplied by higher headquarters. A virtue of American fighting style is that it is far more flexible than what is tolerated in other armed forces, appearing to past enemies as a kind of violent, semiorganized chaos. But that flexibility is *not* chaos; it is based on a concept, and the concept is based on a set of data and on doctrine. And, historically, the whole procedure works pretty well.

The Soviets rely on SOP (or doctrine) far more heavily than we do, and it tends to be used more rigidly, which is handy if you have to slug it out with them, because they can often be counted on to do the predictable thing. At NTC, Soviet doctrine is used in the roughest, toughest, most flexible way the OPFOR commander can manage, but a visitor who has done his homework will have a limited range of problems to worry about when he fights the 32d Guards. And while the Soviet style may have its limitations, ours does too; as a Russian general once remarked,

Graphics are posted in the "Blue" TOC shortly before an order is given. Orders are prepared by the operations officer and his staff using a combination of SOP and the commander's guidance.

Americans write great orders but rarely follow them.

WARNING ORDER

For American forces there is a classic sequence of orders, which are received from above and transmitted to subordinates. The initial orders may be designed and written by people thousands of miles from the sound of guns, with no direct knowledge of the people or the team whose lives they commit to battle. The sequence of orders begins with an alert that a mission is being planned for the unit. This alert is formally called a warning order, which is basically a "heads up" that starts the unit thinking about going to work. The warning order can be given minutes, hours, or days before the formal order. For this

rotation, the initial warning order is written late on Day Two while the troops are still getting the equipment squared away. It trickles down from brigade commander to the battalions, from the battalions to the companies, from the companies to the platoons, and ultimately to the soldiers.

A warning order for a tank platoon comes from the platoon leader, normally a second lieutenant, and is issued to the tank commanders, usually sergeants, whom the platoon leaders gather together. It sounds something like:

Warning order for 3d Platoon—we will con-

The new AH-64 Apache has begun to change the way the game is played at NTC. The Apache is a dedicated armor killer, designed for the attack role. It can appear from nowhere and engage tanks far beyond the enemy's effective range, turning the tables on the OPFOR.

duct an attack to seize a hill at grid Echo Sierra five zero niner three zero six at zero seven hundred hours tomorrow. No movement before zero seven hundred hours. Ammunition and fuel will arrive at twenty-one hundred hours today. Hot chow at zero four hundred hours tomorrow. Precombat inspection at zero four thirty hours tomor-

row. I will issue the operations order at my tank at twenty-two hundred hours tonight.

It is brief, but important because it defines what the mission will be, the earliest time that movement can be expected, and when and where the full order will be given.

OPERATIONS ORDER

While the troops are laboring over the tracks and other gear under the relentless sun, the planners at each level are busy getting ready to execute the warning order. In the tactical operations center currently set up in the Dust Bowl congregate the commanders who receive the complete operations order, a much more detailed elaboration of the warning order.

At the appointed hour the order itself is given. It comes from the next higher unit—brigade orders battalion, battalion orders company, company orders platoon. Each commander receives the order and passes it on to his subordinate leaders, who each do the same in turn.

The order is given in a classic five-paragraph format, which has been in use since cavemen beat on each other with clubs. It begins with the situation, then the mission, then execution, then service support, and finally command and signal. Everybody knows the format, everybody knows the sequence, nobody knows how the battle will actually occur. But this is the best that can be done to organize the human and equipment resources, and focus them on the task at hand.

The *situation:* first, the enemy forces. Exactly who are they, what kind of unit is it, what kind of equipment do they have, and where are they? How strong are they, where are they located, where are their kill zones, how capable are they, and what are they likely to do?

Then the friendly side: what is our mission, the missions of the adjacent units on the left and right, to the front and the rear?

Then the *mission* in detail: a clear, concise statement of what the unit is to do, to include the usual who, where, when, and why of the operation.

The *execution:* what is the concept of the operation? This statement explains how the unit is to maneuver, how it fires, how it deals with obstacles. It is the leader's tactical plan. In offensive operations, it specifies the unit's formation, movement technique, routes of advance, and plans for direct and indirect fire and overwatch. In the defense, it specifies battle positions, weapons orientation, engagement plan, and movement plan for subsequent positions. Artillery support is explained so the unit leaders can anticipate how they will be supported. If individual tanks or units have special assignments, here is where they are defined.

Then come coordinating instructions, which include details for the conduct of the road march, preparation for defense against gas attack, and any other "be prepared" missions.

The fourth item of the order describes what is called *service support,* which is the details of supply and support. Where will refueling happen, and how? Where will the collection point for damaged vehicles be? Where and when will collection points for the dead and wounded be set up? Where will the POW cage be set up?

The final portion of the order, *command and signal,* defines how communications will be maintained and what the succession of command will be when the commander becomes, as they say, "ineffective."

If you were the commander, you'd know the

Soviet forces are coming your way. You've been told that you are to execute a movement to contact. Your mind is full of questions and apprehensions. In the distance you might hear the muted thunder of a massive Soviet artillery barrage, and the smoke of burning vehicles might darken the distant horizon. Our vehicles or theirs? There is no telling, but you have to think it is many of both. At moments like these, soldiers are afraid, and so are their leaders. But to be effective, you will have to retain control—first, of yourself, because leaders are the key to effective preparation, and second, of your people and your equipment.

At the appointed hour the Blue force commanders gather at the tactical operations center, universally known as the TOC. They are tired, and they are dirty.

The TOC is a little headquarters operation, essentially made up of three M113 armored personnel carriers parked together. One belongs to the S2 (intelligence) shop, one to the FIST and the artillery team, and one to S3 (operations). The whole assembly is draped with camouflage nets and embellished with antennas. A generator hums away nearby, and vehicles are parked in clusters in the immediate vicinity. There is an electric coffee pot going, as it always is if the TOC has been in the same spot for more than a few hours.

As the hour for the operations order briefing approaches, the map boards are set up for the inspection of the troop leaders. Preparation of the maps has taken the S3 shop several hours to complete. There are overlays and overlays for the overlays. The phase lines are drawn in and a panel with frequencies and code words is filled in with grease pencil. What will the official

time of first and last light be tomorrow? How much illumination will the moon provide tonight? What will the code word be that tells us to mask against chemical agents? What will be the all-clear?

When a landscape becomes a battlefield, this vision is formalized in important ways on the maps that all the unit leaders carry. Every leader annotates his map with colored markers to assist in navigation and fighting. The map acquires battle positions, phase lines, preplanned artillery targets, terrain reference points, objectives.

The lieutenants and captains filter in under the net and carefully begin to make the notes they will rely on during the operation. They copy the information on the map to their own, crowding around the map and peering at details. In this business, a lot depends on details.

The commander shows up. Depending on his personal style and the circumstances of the moment—both of which vary widely—the mood may be somber or jovial. He begins:

Tank commanders, you are here to receive an operation order. I will tell you the mission-essential information and procedures that differ from our SOP. Hold your questions until I am finished with the entire order.

The situation is as follows: The enemy consists of one mechanized rifle regiment equipped with T-64 or T-72 tanks, BMPs, and BRDMs. The enemy has helicopters and local air superiority. He has been attacking toward the west for the last forty-eight hours and is at approximately 70 percent strength. He has used tactical, nuclear, and chemical weapons. The enemy is tired, his morale is poor, and he is low on all classes of supply. He has temporarily halted in the vicinity of Wolfsbuch and Pondorf, but he is expected

Out by the Racetrack a visiting M1A1 commander takes the late afternoon sun while awaiting the next order. There is no really comfortable spot to rest in a tank.

to continue to advance along two avenues of approach.

The company's mission is to defend from Battle Position 12A no later than 1800 hours tonight. On order, counterattack.

We will accomplish our mission as follows: The scouts will make initial contact, and fall back through contact points 1 and 4, and Battle Position 12C. Once the scouts have cleared 4, 2d Platoon will crater the road. The enemy will advance along both avenues of approach until he nears Winden. At Winden, he will break off and bypass to the north and south of the town. We will fight the element that bypasses to the north. We will begin our engagements once the enemy has at least seven armored vehicles north

of Winden and is in engagement area CAT. We will continue to fight from Battle Position 12A until ordered to move or until the enemy has successfully crossed the obstacles with more than ten tanks.

The time is now 0305 hours. Are there any questions?

When it all comes down to business, every soldier in every unit of the fighting part of the United States Army knows by heart a simple little summary of what he and his compadres have to do; as they say, it's "shoot, scoot, and communicate!"

Movement to Contact

On Day Three of the rotation the action begins. The first mission is the road march. Wake up is 0430, then personal hygiene (the last shower for a while), the last of the hot-water shaves, and breakfast. It's off to the tracks and at 0600 everybody cranks. Only one of the tracks in your platoon needs to get slaved off. After the traditional wait, the lead elements move out and head off into the desert. One at a time, they are joined by tanks and tracks and wheeled vehicles, the rumble of hundreds of engines and tracks filling the air with noise and then with an incredible dust cloud. If you are unlucky, you find yourself on the back of the column.

The MILES systems are up and there is ammunition fed into the guns. We're tactical! The rotation has begun. Nobody is really expecting to get bushwhacked driving out of main post, which probably means that one of these days the OPFOR will try it. But it doesn't happen today, and although everybody is keyed up and glad to be moving, there is still the sense that the tests will not happen until later. The op order said not to expect action until later this afternoon, but to be ready all day.

The road march sounds simple, but often isn't. Moving a battalion of armor, mech infantry, and support vehicles anywhere, on any road, takes planning, a good SOP, time, and teamwork. When the place is the dust and heat of the desert and when it's still dark, a lot can go wrong—and does. A thousand vehicles move out of the Dust Bowl, the roar of exhaust and clatter of tracks making a tremendous din. Tank crews

Lieutenant Colonel Monza checks his map while watching his tanks charge toward the defending 3d Armored Cavalry Regiment near Chinaman's Hat.

sit for hours at their stations, engines idling, waiting for their turn to pull out and into line. The dust is amazing, even before you get off the ''hardball'' road. It fills the air and coats everything. Armor crewmen know to use the large triangular bandage they are issued to make a pretty good dust mask, and almost everyone looks like a mean, green bandito.

Back in the Star Wars building the computer display screens show a god's-eye view of Fort Irwin, with the Dust Bowl centered. Tiny blue symbols are jammed together on the road; if you are lucky enough to share the air-conditioned chill, you will not see the clouds of dust or feel the heat. Like some omniscient god, you can look down on the task force as it moves out, and you can even identify individual vehicles in the parade. The interval between tanks begins to open up a little as drivers make allowance for the dust and the decreased visibility. For hours the train rumbles out of lovely downtown Fort Irwin. The sun settles over the western mountains, and twilight settles on the desert. In the tracks, however, the only thing to be seen is a gradually deepening gloom that progresses from a bright orange to a purple light, then quickly to deep darkness. The tanks and other vehicles all have headlights, but none of them will be turned on; this is a tactical environment, with the forces of evil abroad in the land. The drivers are all expected to be proficient at navigating under such conditions. The night-vision devices are all cranked up to Warp Nine, and each vehicle struggles to maintain interval and stay on the trail.

Although the drivers have work to do, the rest of the crews struggle with boredom and fatigue and the rolling motion of the vehicles. Some nod off to sleep. But the commanders of task forces, battalions, companies, platoons, and tanks all are left to contemplate the ticking of the clock. Somewhere in the dark, far to the west (according to the S2) is a large concentration of enemy armor, and the intel report promises contact within hours. About a third of the task force is composed of leaders, and this is the time for leaders to wonder: What have I overlooked? What have I forgotten? What will the other guy do? How will I perform? How will we perform? But for most of them, the time for questions is past, and it is nearly time for action.

There are still a few people with lots of questions. On the reverse slope of a little cluster of hills thirty kilometers to the west, huddled around a map in the tactical operations center of the 32d Guards Motorized Rifle Regiment, the commander, his intel officer (S2), and his executive officer conspire about the battle they are about to begin. They have already put scouts on hilltops where the enemy can be watched, and while the visitors struggle to stay awake and move through the darkness, their progress is reported at regular intervals. The OPFOR electronic warfare unit is listening to any transmissions the task force is making, and soon will know who the commanders are by call sign and location. The OPFOR S2 shop collects and summarizes all these data for its commander, a tall, dark, not really very handsome guy who is a master at defeating visiting units.

"Well, cowboy, now what do you think he's gonna do?" the commander inquires of the young lieutenant S2. Although thousands of soldiers will face off against each other tonight, the character and intellect of only two of them will have

O/Cs watch as the forces move toward collision. The upper screen is from a video camera on one of the peaks; the other shows a computer-generated map with all the units engaged in the fight.

a profound influence on the battle, and these two are the opposing commanders, each of whom tries to psychoanalyze the other. Each will constantly be alert to clues about the other's style and SOP. While the battle evolves, each tries to anticipate the other's moves, like opposing chess players.

Back in the Star Wars building, the analysts are settling in for another exciting couple of hours. Their screens show the progress of the brigade on the road march, and one of the mech infantry analysts notices something curious developing: The screen shows that the march is interrupted in the middle, that the vehicles toward the back of the column are stopped and bunched up. In the dust and dark a fuel truck and another one of the support vehicles have crunched into

each other; one is already out of the fight. It takes a few minutes to clear the road and to get people moving again.

Out on the desert, the observer/controllers set up shop in their assigned positions or ride alongside the units they are supposed to shadow. Each commander is shadowed by an officer of equal rank who watches and will coach each leader. It is not an especially thankful job, rather like that of a referee in a less deadly game. The O/Cs are like the OPFOR in that they spend tremendous amounts of time out here in the desert and have become masters at maintaining a reasonable level of comfort. Some stock their vehicles with favorite junk food while others stick to Diet Dr. Pepper.

The only enemy involved in the road march is the potential for chaos inherent in moving such a large number of people and vehicles under conditions of darkness and dust and over completely unfamiliar terrain. Every mission has an objective, and this one is a location out past the Valley of Death, beyond the John Wayne Hills, not too far from Siberia. It is not defended real estate, so the task force doesn't expect to have to fight for it, but it has to get there. The commander has planned that the trip should take five hours, and for some of the lead elements, it takes only six. But with one thing and another, the rear-guard elements don't make it in until eight or nine hours after departing, and this is a problem already. The force has to refuel and set up security; people have to maintain vehicles,

An O/C cuts loose with a blast of laser light from his "God gun," zapping a careless M1 that has just stumbled into its own minefield. Such errors are common at the beginning of rotations, less so later on.

eat, sleep, and prepare to receive the next mission. The delay on the road march has altered the carefully considered plans of the task force commander, who doesn't say a thing but is wondering already if he's leading 3,500 soldiers into a disaster.

The TOC is set up in the middle of the assembly area and in the early hours of the morning becomes host to a gathering of commanders who filter in to receive their first combat mission of the war. The latecomers look bedraggled and annoyed at their long ordeal on the road, glad to be finally in the assembly area, but a bit apprehensive. The business of the accident is not a big deal in itself, but it does screw things up, throw off the schedule, and lower the confidence level all around.

FIRST BATTLE

The task force already feels the eyes of the

A Cobra gunship departs on a "cavalry" mission, guarding an observation helicopter that will go looking for trouble. The cav mission for Army air is an important part of armor operations.

OPFOR on them. Across the desert somewhere is a screening force for a Soviet motorized rifle division. The screening force can be identified as belonging to a division because it is known to contain tanks. It also has BMPs and BRDM scout cars stashed here and there in the Valley of Death. There are three in Langford Valley and two in the Valley of Death, each with observation posts tucked into convenient spots to watch and wait. This screen will be waiting for the task force to make its move, then report their dispositions and composition and try to predict where the main effort will come. The Blue commander has long since deployed his scouts, both on the ground and in the air. Out on the desert, far from the assembly area, scout APCs tiptoe around, dropping off OPs (observation posts) and peering through the gloom with their night vision goggles and ground radar.

At 0600 on Day Four the cavalry troop moves out to develop the enemy situation, leading the task force, which is deployed in a loose diamond formation that spreads across several kilometers of real estate. A movement to contact (remember?) is a dangerous maneuver, and you want to make contact with the minimum force possible and still be able to be effective without getting killed off. That's what cavalry is good for—being out front, scooting and snooping. Cavalry is supposed to be light and quick, able to find and fix the enemy and report where his screen and main defenses are. They have three platoons of Bradleys, fourteen vehicles, to work with, and if they do their stuff, they should be able to get past the outposts, mix it up a little with the main defenses, and call back to the boss before going to ground or getting killed. The troop is extremely

cautious, however, and three hours later has moved only three or four kilometers, hasn't really found a thing, and has been reduced by one, which had been bushwhacked by a TOW missile launched from somewhere on the long hill called the Whale.

Back at the screens in the Star Wars building, the cav is represented by little blue symbols, and one now has a black box around it, showing its death from a direct-fire weapon. Another monitor lists the shot that killed it, by time, position, weapon type, and effect. The analysts are just about going to sleep; the cav is taking too much time, but this is not unusual in first engagements.

By 1030 the cavalry has found the screen for the OPFOR main defensive positions and the battle is joined. The mechanized infantry task force is following the cavalry into the Whale

OPFOR engineers from the 7th Infantry Division (Light) dash from their APC to breach an obstacle in front of the advance.

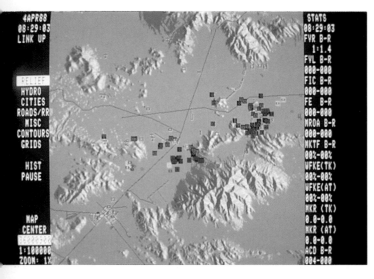

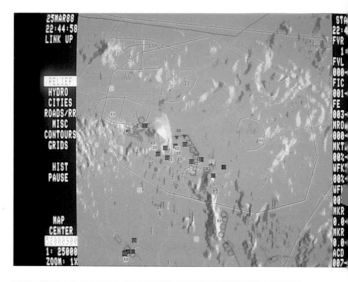

A god's-eye view of battle. The blue boxes are friendly armor, the red belong to enemy, and the black boxes show kills. Black lines show roads, and that's Fort Irwin's main post in the lower left.

Large irregular blue circles show use of smoke by the visiting "Blue" forces. The red circles and lines show razor-wire concertina obstacles emplaced by OPFOR engineers.

Gap, a dangerous place where tanks are forced to travel. Since it is a predictable travel destination, the OPFOR have targeted it for preplanned artillery missions. Although two of the 32d Guards vehicles have been killed, a scout car up a little wadi overlooking the gap is calling in artillery and providing adjustments that begin to kill vehicles in the Blue task force. While some of the force tries to blast through the gap, others take the high ground just to the right of it—Furlong Ridge. They've already lost three Bradleys and a tank, all to artillery. The numerous wadis that cut through the desert provide ready-made defensive positions, obstacles, and hidden highways for soldiers smart enough to use them, and the OPFOR are smart enough.

The Blue air cavalry squadron flying in support of the mission spots what it believes is a large concentration of enemy vehicles in the vicinity of hill 466, and the task force FIST calls for a fire mission on the area. Back in the Star Wars building, the analysts tasked with watching for such events yell "ARTILLERY!" as their screens show the symbols for fire missions. On the ground north of the Whale Gap, the observer/controllers who serve as fire markers shoot artillery simulators on the appointed spots. The area is saturated, but there are no kills. The concentration seen by the air cav scouts did not exist. A few vehicles moving in the dust seemed much more, and a lot of effort was wasted. This is not unusual. The main body of the Blue force sits tight and waits timidly to see what happens. At 1050 a Sagger missile fired by a BMP kills

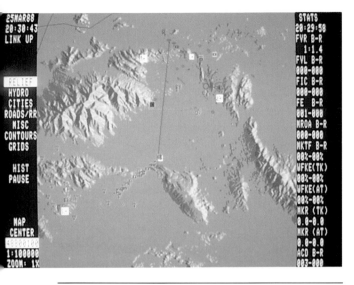

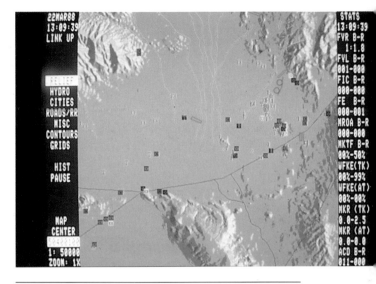

Artillery! The red line shows a self-propelled howitzer firing into the massed visitors as they try to force their way through the tiny Whale Gap. The survivors will continue to be engaged as they flood across the open ground to the north.

Many dead vehicles are scattered across the battlefield, although the Blue forces have retained a significant amount of combat power as they continue to press toward the enemy.

another Bradley; less than a minute later, the screens show the BMP engaged by a tank, which kills it.

The main body of the Blue force is sent through the Whale Gap toward the enemy position that has been identified by the cav. Artillery pounds the gap as the vehicles race through, killing several tanks and other vehicles. The O/Cs zoom around the battle, bravely oblivious to the laser beams zipping through the dust, but damn careful to avoid getting squished under the tracks of the squirming and racing M1s and Bradleys. The fire markers toss their artillery simulators on command, then draw their "god gun" and zap the tanks the computer says are now dead.

Inside the vehicles, the crews, tired from the days of anticipation and movement, are momen-

tarily pumped up by a triple dose of adrenaline as they try to squirm through the carnage, avoid other vehicles (living and dead), identify bad guys, and shoot at them.

"GUNNER! SABOT! BMP, RIGHT FRONT, 300 METERS!" yells the commander of an M1.

The turret motor whines as the gun rotates quickly to the right. "IDENTIFIED!" yells the gunner.

"UP!" the loader reports.

The commander is glued to his sight. "FIRE!"

"ON THE WAY!" is the response, and a Hoffman charge fires over the main gun. Through the dust a bright yellow light flashes on the top of a VISMOD BMP. There is a chorus of cheers from the tank crew, but it is quickly replaced by a loud, continuous tone from a speaker inside the turret, clearly audible to all. The strobe light on the M1 is flashing, too; the victor has been vanquished as well.

"OH, NO!" yells the commander. Then, to the loader, "SEE WHAT KILLED US." The loader checks the little panel on the MILES system that shows a kill code, and the sad news is that while thrashing around with the BMP the M1 has blundered into a mine field, one that had been well marked. A controller had been watching for just such inattention, and zapped the tank with the god gun. For many of the task force it is a short battle, but not a sweet one.

The survivors move to engage the defending enemy forces, trying to avoid the obstacles built by OPFOR engineers. The slow progress of the task force permits the OPFOR to drench the force with artillery and direct fire, and it is not long before the leading elements are parked in disar-

After the battle: a crew poses with its faithful steed near Langford Lake while waiting for the order to "reconstitute."

78

Lieutenant Colonel Hedgpeth is the senior O/C for Blue air, and has "killed" one of the Hueys for flying too close to Red antiair defenses.

ray, kill lights flashing and gun tubes lowered. The crews sit on the hulls of their chariots, helmets off, watching the show from the sidelines.

By 1300 the task force has been whittled down to the point where it can't accomplish its mission; they've been whipped on their first fight. The brigade and task force (TF) commanders huddle at the TOC. The TF commander has to report that he does not have sufficient combat power remaining to attack the enemy defensive belt. The commanders conclude that it's time to pull

back and establish a hasty defense. The word from above is that the enemy is preparing to launch a major offensive, and the new mission will be to establish a defense in sector.

When the dust finally settles, the controllers come along to rekey the MILES systems on people and tank weapon systems, permitting them to return to the war. While the troops are recover-

The sun sets on Day Four near Siberia. A tank gunner considers his options for the morrow when a regiment of bad guys will test the visitors.

Captain Williams provides the after-action review for a group of platoon officers who've just discovered what NTC is all about.

ing from the experience, the O/Cs are preparing the first after-action review. The commanders go off to the AAR van to see videotaped highlights and to participate in discovery learning. (Can you say "total disaster," boys and girls? Sure you can!) Each gets up in turn and briefly describes what he and his people did well, and what they need to work at. Here, for the first time, they see how the actual battle evolved and who did what to whom. For some, it can be a surprise and a revelation. Orders that went out over the air sometimes sound very different when replayed in the AAR than they were remembered by the guy who spoke them into the mike. The first battle is an intense learning experience, and a kind of trauma, but it is only the first of many.

The senior O/C leads the session, and he is low key about the whole thing. The tapes and the summary from the computer display show the leaders everything they need to know. The AAR is essentially an instant replay of the battle in detail, and nobody has to be told that they screwed up—they already know and can see it on the silver screen. Every leader participates in turn. Each identifies his unit's successes and failures.

Away from the group, one of the senior O/Cs critiques this first battle:

The problems with this mission were that first, the time used by the cav to execute a zoned reconnaissance was excessive. The cav didn't function as an advance guard for the main body; they stopped too soon, failed to take out the screen elements, and didn't really identify the main defensive belt. This prevented the main force from going over the top of the Whale. The TF lost its formation going through the gap and never got back together to regain command and control. They lost all of the scouts forward, so there were not a lot of eyes forward to tell the commander what was going on and where the enemy was. As combat power was lost, the commander lost the ability to mount a hasty attack. For the kind of movement-to-contact engagements we see out here, it took longer than normal; for a first mission, it was about average in terms of results. Movement to contact is the hardest mission a TF commander has to do because he has little or no intelligence about the enemy, and it is the first mission out of the starting blocks so that makes it doubly tough. This happens to a lot of visiting units—they get through the screen and establish contact with the main defense, but then lose combat power and are unable to take any kind of offensive action. He lost about 50 percent of his power in the engagement. In our

82

fundamentals of what we call the AirLand Battle there are four elements: agility, initiative, depth, and synchronization. Synchronization means that we try to mass our combat power with our artillery, smoke, aviation, and put all those elements together at the same time. It didn't happen today.

The AARs for the tankers are given in the dirt overlooking the fight. The emphasis is on the positive lessons of the experience, what went right and what to do the next time to make everything come out better. Just the same, there is a feeling of failure and defeat in the air.

"Well, we screwed the pooch today!" says one young tanker. "We didn't get off a single shot."

Soon the S2 and S3 staffs are getting ready for round two with the red horde, and the intel coming down warns of a major attack by a full motorized rifle regiment. The young NCOs and officers who will brief the commanders prepare the overlays in the familiar way. Refueling trucks show up at the appointed places and resupply begins for machines and people.

The tired troopers would like to sleep, but they have work to do instead. The leaders gather at the TOC again, dusty and dragging from the day's fight, to receive another mission, while the crews maintain the tracks and take care of resupply. According to the intelligence report from Corps, the task force will have to defend against a Soviet attack that will try to push through the area they now occupy. There is little time and much to do.

Two junior enlisted men overwatch the battlefield where so many visiting units have been destroyed.

Defend in Depth

Out on the desert, defending and attacking forces probe and observe, preparing for the next fight. On hillsides and in the wadis are the recon teams watching for movement and creeping around in search of barriers. The radio net comes alive with the business of preparation. The OPFOR and Blue electronic warfare units strain to find the pattern, to find the location of the units, to discover the enemy plan for the battle to come.

Back at the TOC site, the unit leaders congregate to see the picture being painted on the situation and the mission they will share tomorrow.

The S2 tells the leaders that they think four or five dismounted two-man observation teams have been inserted already on high ground overlooking their positions, and that these teams will be trying to report back on where and how the TF will defend. This means that the counterrecon battle has already begun, and tired scouts are already out searching for the OPFOR.

Of course the units in the TF have a sleep plan that should get everybody at least four hours rest in every twenty-four, but leaders often try to tough it out for a few days, to make sure everything gets done. It isn't unusual for people to go seventy-two hours without more than a catnap or two. There are a couple of these guys at the orders briefing and they are counseled to get some rest.

The order is presented in its usual formal manner, by a tired S2 to the assembled multitude: "Okay, gentlemen, let's get started here. We'll get this thing over with, then ask your questions

and you can get back to your units." He goes through the standard business about time zone, task organization, sunrise, and sunset; then the interesting part begins:

Enemy forces: the 19th Combined Arms Army is expected to launch an attack to seize objectives around East Gate Pass. Force used may be operational detachment of motorized rifle regiment (reinforced). Dismounted recon teams have been reported in sector. Anticipate 300 dismounted infantry to infiltrate tonight. Expect a full regimental attack tomorrow morning around first light; defend in sector, stand to at 0430, be prepared to go to MOPP 4 [full chemical protection suit and mask] *early. They will probably gas us. Do not unmask until you get the official word!*

They all pay close attention and take copious notes.

Commander's intent: the commander intends to destroy an MRR [motorized rifle regiment] *in sector by* defending in depth. *His operation is divided into three phases:*

In phase one, India troop during the hours of darkness and the air cavalry troop during daylight conduct a screen along PL (phase line) Pleasanton, engaging enemy recon elements with indirect fires and reporting the main attack.

In phase two, the squadron will assist the regiment in locating and eliminating enemy recon elements in sector.

The third phase is the main battle. The commander intends to destroy two motorized rifle battalions from positions along PL Apple, then destroy the third battalion with Mike company deep in sector.

The whole briefing takes about an hour, and there are lots of questions. Finally, the leaders depart to their units, where they will pass the

word, rehearse, prepare, plan—and possibly get some sleep.

Desert twilight is early and brief at this time of year. The scouts move forward just after last light, a thumbnail moon and starlight all the illumination anybody has to work with. It is enough for the scouts, who are adept at braille navigation and have radar for eyes. The basic mission of the scouts is to be the commander's eyes on the ground, looking forward. They will insinuate themselves as deeply as they can, hopefully al-

When it's time to defend, the combat engineers can be worth their massive weight in gold. Here they are preparing a fighting position for a tank and will work through the night.

most on top of the enemy. They are a human direct-early-warning radar system, and they are important to the battle, although they may never fire a shot. In fact, scouts aren't supposed to shoot unless they have to save their hide. In the defense, they wait in a screen line within

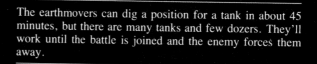

The earthmovers can dig a position for a tank in about 45 minutes, but there are many tanks and few dozers. They'll work until the battle is joined and the enemy forces them away.

artillery range; when the enemy attacks, revealing his size, location, and direction, then the scouts fall back behind the big boys, where it's safe. But tonight they watch for the enemy they know are out there, and when they see them—or think they see them—it is a simple matter to make the call for fire that would dump 155mm rounds on the target. Here, though, O/Cs on the ground use fire markers and god guns to simulate artillery. The 32d Guards will lose some teams tonight, and some will live to accomplish their missions.

During the afternoon the regiment moves into positions around a valley that is called the Colorado on the map, and the scouts move up trails and across country toward the area where the intel shop says the bad guys are. They set up a screen line several klicks forward, moving out in their M113s and slipping the boxy personnel carriers into obscure little folds in the terrain. Ramps drop and out go the troops, who scurry up into the rocks with their rifles, night-vision goggles, and binoculars. They find a spot somewhere between the top and the bottom of a hill, an inconspicuous place suitable for someone who wants to be invisible. The enemy regiment is out there somewhere, and their scouts are prowling around in that same inky darkness looking for us and for our defenses. They will try to find out where our mine fields are and where the tank ditches go, where the wire is and where it isn't; then they will try to find ways around them. They know their business and know the

The 32d Guards move up in preparation for their attack, which will come across the ghastly Washboard. Such road marches raise tremendous clouds of dust and provide great warning for the enemy.

terrain, but we have night-vision devices and they don't. The game would be more fun if everyone wasn't so tired.

The stillness of the air and the open terrain allow sound to travel long distances with great clarity. Engineer vehicles can be heard laboring through the night, preparing defensive positions for our tanks and obstacles for the T-72s and BMPs. But far off, forward where the scouts should be, the familiar but distant rhythm of a machine gun begins to make its music, joined quickly with the pops of rifle fire. Then the gunfire fades away. We've lost one of the outposts already.

While the scouts are trying to remain invisible and tank crews prepare range cards and try to implement sleep plans, one group of people is really just starting to work, and will labor through most nights and many days. They are the engineers, and they are very much part of the action,

although they seldom get the glory. Engineers have a lot to do with movement and survival on the battlefield, and the tanks and the troops would not last very long without their support.

One of the engineer missions, called survivability, involves preparation of fighting positions for the tanks and infantry. You can dig in a tank with an E tool, but it will take a lifetime to do it, which on the battlefield is the length of time required for the other team to show up.

Engineers dig bunkers and battle positions for tanks, and trenches and berms for artillery and crews. During combat operations, they get the unenviable chore of breaching mine fields and opening paths through triple concertina wire. (Since obstacles are normally protected by fire from artillery or small arms, this is not one of

As night falls on the desert, an M1 from the 2d Armored Division hastily repositions, gun tube in trail. Near Brigade Hill, Day Five.

the jobs the recruiters tell you about on your first visit.)

The engineers have two missions in their bag of tricks that are seemingly contradictory. One is called mobility, which involves helping the fighting forces move on the battlefield. The other is called countermobility, which involves slowing or halting the opposing team. This means that the engineers are very familiar with mines, ditches, rivers, and wire, both ours and theirs. And when things get dull and no entertainment

Antiaircraft radar systems used by Threat nations are simulated by this device, which "kills" a lot of careless visiting air assets.

is available, they can always conduct raids and fight as infantry.

While the TF is trying to get its act together, things are busy in a wadi many miles to the west. The OPFOR is going about its business with quiet professionalism. The OPFOR tactical operations center is stashed neatly behind a low hill, the three APCs cuddled up close to each other and the whole melange draped with cammo nets that match the color and texture of the surroundings extremely well. Up close you can spot the TOC by the little forest of antennas that poke through the nets, but you need to be looking for them. Inside the S2 track is a large pot of fresh coffee that sustains the cast of characters who work nearby. One of the tracks is owned by the OPFOR FIST, the artillery fire-support team. The third belongs to the engineers. Both are busy plotting and scheming, working their magic and planning for a happy tomorrow.

It isn't quite time for the OPFOR briefing, but the players are starting to show up. One is the commander of the scout unit. His people have been busy: ''I take the teams in my BRDMs out at night, like I did last night. I take them deep and drop them off at the base of a hill; they go on top of the hill and they hide, and they observe. All morning they have been observ-

Sgt. Gordon Tom, gunner on tank Fox 22, on his second NTC rotation.

95

ing and sending back reports. We put out eight teams, and six are still alive; they took out two. A lot of the visiting units put in their obstacles at night because our deep recon teams are daylight only; we don't have night-vision devices like they do.''

Another of the OPFOR players is the electronic warfare (EW) officer. Some of the antennas that poke out of the camouflage netting belong to the electronic warfare section, a batch of cheerful people who have more fun than just about anybody. They get to listen to the radio traffic from the other guys, they get to jam it, and when they are feeling frisky, they call up the enemy for a friendly chat.

The job of the EW folks is to replicate Soviet EW support. They look for any lapses of communications security, and there are always plenty. They use direction finders, an intercept team, and a great big jammer, along with a couple of ground radars up forward. At first they just sit out there and listen, building a list of Blue freqs; then they figure out who is where, and what they intend to do. The EW section is famous for discovering all sorts of things about the visitors' intentions. And, for fun and profit, they will occasionally call up the Blues and play games. ''My unit spends a lot of time in the field; one of the reasons we're so good is that we get a lot of practice. I can always find LD [line of departure] times, scout pushes; you can almost always pick up those guys talking,'' says

On the back side of the Peanut a T-72 fires a Hoffman charge at a retreating M1. Although a blank, it is still dangerous out to about 50 feet.

the EW officer. "That's immediate feedback about what the enemy is going to do."

Then there are the engineers. You can always pick them up and figure out where the mine fields and wire are going. And there are the chow trucks; they will show you where the soldiers are. I will listen to anything and everything. They give away the locations of artillery and battle positions for the tanks. We use the direction finders to locate the emitters and that reveals the positions.

We get our best intel at night when the guys

A visiting Marine tries out the medium antitank weapon that is replacing the LAW. It's still not big enough to take out a T-80 with one shot, but it has lots of uses on the battlefield just the same, and is a big improvement.

are locked in the vehicles and they have to use their radios, and when they use the radios they emit a signal, and with a little luck I'll be there listening for 'em. Then we try to make sense of it all, then pass it on to the Two [the S2 intel officer] who will use it as part of the briefing for the Old Man. Here, vehicles come with ra-

dios; anybody can talk on the radio . . . we believe in "press to talk." Because of that, anybody can violate the security of the net—and they do, all the time.

This particular visiting unit has rather bad communications security, and are giving away a lot to the OPFOR.

These guys talk a lot. Lousy comsec! They use bogus call signs, so you can identify them very quickly. JEDI 6 happens to be the commander of the 4th Aviation Squadron, the combat aviation squadron. I'll follow his call sign

An M60 from the 197th Brigade moves to engage a Hind attacking his unit. The reverse side of a slope provides some cover, until it's time to jump up and fire. The main gun is excellent against such threats if they are in range.

through frequency changes for the next fourteen days. And he's going to tell me exactly what I need to know. And if I feel like having fun, I'll wait till he leaves the net, and call up one of his guys, and say "This is JEDI 6; reposition helicopters south; we have a breakthrough of an MRB here."

99

The OPFOR regimental commander shows up at the TOC while the preparation for the order is going on. The commander makes the final decision, but not before a lot of people help him make it. They influence him by providing information and counsel. At the moment the S2—everybody just calls him the Two—is briefing the commander on the latest intel from the scouts and the other sources.

The commander stares intently at the map laid out before him and turns to his XO: "All right, John, what do you want to do? The first decision is: do we go *dispersed,* or do we go as a *regiment?* I think the S2's assumption is correct, that we're back with a tank company that will defend back here, and then one that will sit in here. And they're ready to go either way. And they probably run the squadron boundaries something like this . . . he's got some tanks in here, probably keep his tank platoons deep . . . these platoons are

gonna go forward and come back with 'em . . . they're gonna maneuver with him, so as far as the eighteen tanks go, they're gonna stay up here, and then we've got the twenty-eight that are gonna face us in the back in groups of fourteen. So whaddya wanna do, Hero?"

"Here's the thing," says the XO, "whatever happens, we're all gonna end up in the same spot."

"You got it! We all gotta go to the tanks!"

"So the question becomes, how fast do you want to get there, as opposed to how *confused* do you want to make him?"

"With tanks in the rear, confusion becomes

An M163A1 Vulcan is a 20mm six-barreled cannon. It can engage aerial targets to 1,200 meters, ground targets (troops, support vehicles, and very light armor) to 2,000 meters.

more important to me. He knows I've only got two avenues of approach, or maybe three. That's what he knows. He can therefore conceivably take this tank company, if I go north, and move it over here, this way. And if I go south, he takes this company and moves it around the back. Let's figure he's smarter than we are."

"Here's what we gotta avoid: we gotta avoid being attrited to the point where we run into the mass of his M1s."

"Ah! But what do we have to avoid attriting? Can't lose my tanks early!"

"Right! We've got to get across Barstow Road with at least two MRBs, and once we hit Barstow Road, if he is down here, the best place to be is up here. Make him attack uphill at us, but the question is, how do we get there? If I go regimental, I go north and straight on back. I say, come on up and get me! I avoid his squadron in the south and the attrition down south. If I come at him frontally, to confuse him, what we have to weigh is how much that is going to buy us. So, if you go frontally, you stagger your LD times, make sure two MRBs come together at this point to get to the final objective. One MRB is going to have a long way, working through the washboard, but these come out early, they're confusing him."

SECOND BATTLE

At 0530 scouts on hill 781 report a tremendous number of OPFOR vehicles moving toward the defending TF. The commander has positioned a company team on top of the Whale, with tanks and Bradleys; a tank team on the reverse of Furlong Ridge; a tank team in a horseshoe defensive formation between OP Juanita and OP2; a mechanized infantry team in the Valley of Death, with M1s and Bradleys; and an antitank company in two positions, at OP1 and OP2. They are out of range of each other, so they will not be able to provide supporting fires. There are almost no tank ditches or wire obstacles to impede the attacking forces. But the Blue commander expects the attack to be forced into the Whale Gap where the massed fires of artillery and direct fire weapons (tank guns and missiles) should be able to destroy the OPFOR. As the battle is joined, the OPFOR hears their leader's distinctive voice over the net: "Okay, guys, be a hero. Kill them!"

It doesn't take long for the TF to find that the other guys have a different game plan: The company in the Valley of Death is promptly killed by artillery and the infantry, one of the companies defending the gap is dead to artillery, gas has been delivered into the area, and the Red Horde is swarming over the top of the Whale rather than through the gap. An hour after the attack begins, the defenders are down to 50 percent of their starting combat power. The deep defenders are taking losses, and infantry is swarming over the position of the team in the north while the commander desperately tries to reposition his survivors. Only the antitank company stands between the OPFOR and its objective—twelve TOW vehicles against one hundred forty tanks and fighting vehicles. The TOWs can kill well, when properly used in depth and detail, but that doesn't happen today.

The OPFOR commander stands in the hatch of his tank, watching the battle develop from his vantage point on a hillside. He keys his microphone and sends a heads up to one of his tank units, using the dehydrated format required by radio procedure. The commander's job now is to coach his team and coordinate information with the plan about the evolving fight and still provide enough control to make things go the way they're supposed to. All he has now is his experience, his character, and a radio mike with a button on the side. His call sign is XRAY and he now has a success to exploit if he can:

"OSCAR [the call sign of one of the companies], XRAY. WATCH THE GOAT TRAIL; WE'RE KILLING STUFF UP THERE. YOU STILL GOT YOUR PEOPLE ON SITE?"

"AFFIRMATIVE!" is the reply. "I'VE GOT M1S APPROACHING BATTLE POSITION FOUR ALPHA ROMEO FOX FOUR FIVE [a map location concealed over the radio with temporary coordinates]."

Of the three battalions that the TF defended against, only one was killed, and the rest succeeded in the attack. All that stands between the OPFOR and the no-penetration line of the defenders is one cavalry troop with a handful of vehicles deep in sector. But the cav redeems itself today and becomes highly effective at killing the OPFOR, eliminating about as many of the enemy as the entire mechanized infantry component of the TF. They are well dug in, have a good indirect fire plan, and have rehearsed themselves for just this moment. They are faced with what is called a target-rich environment, and as the enemy come in range, right in his carefully planned engagement area, the cav commander gives an unusual order:

"ON MY COMMAND—FIRE!"

All eleven Bradleys fire at once and the attackers are suddenly confused and out of action, strobe lights flashing. Well, at least somebody in the TF seems to be learning something!

Day Eight, Central Engagement Corridor. An exhausted and frustrated senior officer from the 3d ACR waits for yet another briefing as the rotation takes its toll. Commanders are the most likely to ignore the sleep plan.

The after-action review starts early today. The net effect was not too hot—the commander made some errors—but there were signs of progress. The TF is still too dispersed and not providing mutual support. The first thing that should have been done was to look at where the attack could have come, then to plan the defense based on those natural avenues of approach. It didn't happen. The result was that the enemy was able— once again—to deal with the Blue force one element at a time, piecemeal. The OPFOR controlled the fight—until they got to the cav troop. Hard lessons learned the hard way.

Change of Mission

Those who can flop down and are engulfed in a deathlike sleep, drained of energy by the prolonged tension and stress. But there is much work to be done, and tired, stressed people will have to do it. Equipment has broken and must be fixed; fuel and ammunition have been consumed and must be replaced.

The OPFOR elements pull back and establish a defensive zone on the terrain called Siberia. The TF will have thirty-six hours to recover and reconstitute before making a carefully planned assault at 2000 on the ninth day of the rotation.

THIRD BATTLE— DELIBERATE ATTACK, NIGHT

The commander sends out two observation teams—one on the high ground to the east, another to the west—and they send back solid information about the nature of the OPFOR defense. One of the teams gets within a few hundred meters of the enemy, and stays put, reporting back all the latest gossip, right up until the attack. While the OPs are setting up shop, the TF scout platoon is right back out there, snooping and scooting, developing the situation. Unlike the earlier efforts, these are paying off early, with accurate information on the obstacles that the OPFOR engineers are building.

When the attack kicks off, it begins with a call for fire, and the recon effort pays off quickly.

Hasty defensive positions offer little protection as several tank companies recover from one battle and prepare for yet another. Central Engagement Corridor, Day Nine.

The artillery promptly kills three OPFOR vehicles while the TF is crossing the line of departure. Artillery continues to pound the OPFOR positions, spotted by the well-sited OPs. The task force continues its assault, but gradually bunches up a bit, then piles into a large obstacle that hadn't been well marked by the recon team. The TF is held up for fifteen minutes while engineers breach the obstacle, taking three or four losses in the process.

2145: The TF is through the obstacle and spread out over three kilometers.

2215: The TF regains mass at hill 781, and one of the companies succeeds in getting vehicles on the objective.

2245: Two Bradleys breach the defenses and drive on to the objective, but command and control has been lost. Reporting becomes spotty, and the commander doesn't know about the breach and can't help direct forces to exploit it. There are only two BMPs left in the west and the route is essentially open for the taking. But without the report, the TF tries to force its way through and is spread out and loses its mass.

2315: With 50 percent of its power left, the TF has placed elements on the objective, but much of the force has died in the enemy fire sack. The engagement has been a success because of individual initiative of squads and crews, but not a major success because of a loss (again) of command and control. The objective has been secured but not seized. The OPFOR has only about 25 percent of its combat power still alive, so the TF is at least shooting well in the dark. They're improving. After more struggle and sacrifice, the force attains some of its objectives, but is spent in the process. Well, they seem to be catching on here and there.

Here is one area where NTC gets some criticism from old combat tankers: "My experience tells me that any unit that sustains that much damage in an hour-plus period would be totally ineffective, demoralized beyond their ability to recover. It might be okay in training, but it isn't going to be that way in combat."

The after-action review tells the players pretty much what they already know. They are doing better, but it would be nice if they lived to enjoy their victories. After the AAR, the O/C counsels the officers of one company:

A huge M88 tank recovery vehicle gets its tracks tensioned during a lull between battles. Its crew usually cares for the sick and wounded tanks, APCs, and self-propelled howitzers.

You're at the midway point here at the NTC. This is the time when people start getting on each other's nerves. Now, I can tell you guys are friends and you're a good team; the only way you're going to be successful—to continue to be successful—is as a team. You won't win

unless you're on the same team! Okay . . . now, you've got a mission coming up here tomorrow; what do we have to do to get ready for it?

The mech TF moves off to live fire in the north, and receives its mission to defend against a massive attack. This is a decided change of mission, because now everybody puts the MILES transmitters in storage, and the real ammunition gets issued.

LIVE FIRE

There is a rumble off in the distance. Air Force A-10s swoop low and pull up over mountains miles away. Down the road toward the defensive positions roll the tracks from the TF scout platoons as they pull back. Behind them can be seen tanks that pause in their flight to fire at the onslaught. Occasionally a column of smoke will mark a kill seven or more kilometers to the front. From our rear comes the boom of the big 155mm SP howitzers firing over us, a strange rustling sound as the shells pass above our positions. The last of the rear guard slip back into the fold, and a tremendous explosion sends a tower of dust, dirt, and rocks hundreds of feet skyward as the engineers set off several hundred pounds of C4 explosive, cutting the one route through a complicated set of obstacles on the south side of our positions.

Now the enemy tanks are visible in the distance, and occasionally the flash of a main gun

The power packs for tanks and APCs are designed for quick removal and replacement, here assisted by an M88 and its huge hoist.

An OPFOR armored personnel carrier uses smoke to hide while delivering its cargo of engineers to battle.

reveals their engagement of our most forward elements. The advance is startling in its speed. Main guns from tanks nearby crack as the enemy closes to about three kilometers. Soon there is fire coming and going all around us. The M1s wait in their holes for a good opportunity, then pull forward and up just long enough to aim and fire. The concussion of the gun raises a huge cloud of dust around each tank, and soon the air is full of dust and noise. The TOWs, Vulcans, 50-caliber machine guns, mortars, 155mm and 105mm artillery, and rifles all combine to pound the advancing regiment.

"GUNNER! SABOT! TANK, FRONT, 2,000 METERS!"

"IDENTIFIED!"

"UP!"

"FIRE!"

"ON THE WAY!"

Enemy air appears overhead, and the Vulcan air defense system fires repeatedly at the fast mover. They never hit it. Soon there are T-72s and then infantry swarming across the battle position; then they retreat. Slowly, quiet returns to the valley.

Live fire is really exciting, and there isn't anything like it in the rest of the nation. All the vehicles are loaded up with the real thing, not lasers, and the possibilities for accident are quite real. People are in fact shot here from time to time. There is a lot of lead in the air. The attacking tanks, however, are pop-up panels, driven by the big computer that also scores the hits. The illusion of a regiment moving forward is real enough, though. The enemy fast mover is a large model airplane controlled by radio. It swoops provocatively above the battle, Vulcan gunners trying to shoot it down, rarely touching

A VISMOD BMP deep in battle pauses to consider the next move. Hidden Valley, Day Nine.

it. They tend to miss because they like to turn off the radar and aim by eye, and it doesn't usually work very well.

The after-action review for Fox Company is done alongside one of the tanks still in its fighting position. The company's officers are tired and dusty, but they listen to the O/C captain with alert interest. "We've done well today; we did some excellent killing. But there were a couple of areas where we had problems. I want you all to learn from those problems so we can do better next time!"

One of the problems was the company commander's decision to have all the other tanks dug in before his own; when the battle began, he was still sitting out exposed to the enemy. The commander's tank and guidance were both lost almost immediately when the battle was joined, a result of his consideration for his soldiers. "I know you were thinking of your men when you let them get dug in first, but the result

A real TOW missile departs on its mission with a pop and a whoosh. The blue warhead means it's a practice round and won't hurt quite as much if it hits you.

is that they lost you and they lost your leadership right away. You weren't there when they needed you!''

The troop commander and the O/C kick around the problem for a bit, then get on to the next topic, a success. "I saw something out here today that is very rare, something that really impressed us, and that was your two-two tank. It isn't very often that we see a crew with the presence of mind to engage close-in infantry on both sides of their tank with the machine guns while they're still fighting armor with the main gun, but this

An OPFOR T-72 sits dead by the road, killed in the first minutes of the last battle of the rotation. The visitors are finally starting to take apart the OPFOR.

tank did. Very impressive; I'll be mentioning it to the Old Man.''

BRIGADE ATTACK

On Day Ten the mech inf TF returns from live fire to work with the armor TF in brigade-sized engagements, beginning with a movement to contact. Now, this should be interesting; the little puppies are getting tired, and we can see if they've learned anything. Movement to contact (you will recall) is the first mission visitors received, and one of the toughest. This time, both the armor and mech infantry will attack together, with considerably more size and complexity, and that means a more difficult command and control problem for the big boss.

People are tired, dirty, and irritable. This is the point where things can either come together or fall apart. Now is when the O/Cs start looking for the learning curve to go up rapidly—although with some units, it goes the other way.

The TOC is set up again, units go through their routines again. The excitement begins to wear thin under the abrasion of the desert, the

heat and cold, the embarrassing skill of the OPFOR, and all the other irritations that are found in war.

Leaders gather for another briefing, but this time there are more of them, a whole brigades worth. The new mission is to execute a movement to contact with an OPFOR motorized rifle brigade that has set up shop about fifteen miles to the east, part of a divisional element. There will be a divisional and regimental recon screen to be penetrated, and a main defensive belt to be identified. The brigade will follow its cavalry squadron, which will develop the situation, then pass the armor and mech infantry through to

Two BMPs zip past each other in the confusion of a rout, dust and excitement creating the hazard of collision. Despite the wide open spaces, tanks often thrash about in close proximity.

engage the main defense. When the main defense is found, the TF will go to ground while friendly forces prepare to attack.

0500: The cav squadron moves across the line of departure with two cav troops (nineteen Bradleys each), an engineer platoon, and two air cav troops with Cobras and OH58s. Behind them in suitable array are the scouts of the two TFs. Forty minutes behind the leaders come the armor (north) and the mech infantry (south).

0600: The cav makes contact with the OPFOR screen and the fight is on. It doesn't take long before the cav kills off the OPFOR recon element, and the OPFOR commander has suddenly lost much of his information about the evolution of the battle.

0700: The cav gets past the screen and presses on to the main defenses, the scouts and the main body following in good order.

0900: The cav goes to ground in front of the main defensive belt. Their job is now to observe, report, and provide overwatching fires to support the main body, which now passes through the cav's lines and on to find and fight the main defense. The cav once again quits a bit early, out of range of direct engagement fires. But they have developed the situation well, killed well, helped preserve the main force, and stayed alive. The OPFOR squirms and scurries:

"GRID THREE SEVEN ONE SIX, TWELVE PCS AND TEN M1S MOVING WEST, OVER!"

Somewhere in the middle of the brawl, an overexcited OPFOR leader screams into his mike that he's facing thirty-six tanks: "FIVE ZERO, ZERO SIX, HAVE THREE SIX TANGO, EXECUTE FOUR BRAVO! SAY AGAIN, FOUR BRAVO!"

Unfortunately for him, though, he fails to use the right frequency. The commander chimes in: "WRONG NET. YOU'LL NEVER DO IT ON THIS NET."

1000: The armor and mech TFs pass through the cav lines in sync and pretty much intact. The mech TF pushes around to the north, trying to flank the defense and avoiding the OPFOR kill sack in front of the main defensive belt. By 1030 both TFs are in full contact with the defenders and begin to break through. The TF is victorious and the OPFOR withdraws with the Blues in pursuit.

1200: The OPFOR has one MRB left (thirteen tanks and thirty-one BMPS) and the brigade has succeeded in its mission of penetrating the security zone and finding the main defensive belt. At this point the brigade goes to ground for change of mission.

The AAR is considerably more positive on this movement to contact than for the first mission. The elements of the brigade worked together, the cav did its job (even if it stopped a little early), and the OPFOR was soundly defeated by units working together as a team.

NATIONAL TRAINING CENTER AFTER-ACTION REVIEW

People who've been to a rotation at NTC often find that it's a profound experience, changing the way they think about their profession, their

Stand down. The last battle of the rotation over, a 3d ACR tank rumbles back to the Dust Bowl.

units, themselves. They tend to have the enthusiasm of evangelists. Here are just a few comments:

- "This is the only place that you can go and train as if you were on a battlefield. You don't have to worry about anything except your war fighting doctrine with no distractions. You must do everything as you would do it in combat if you intend to succeed out here. If you don't fix a vehicle, it's not going to be ready to fight the next day. If you don't provide security for your logistics package that's coming forward with your food and your fuel and ammunition, and it gets attacked, then you don't have it for the next day. If you forget to requisition ammunition, then you are out of luck. There is NOTHING that stops the action here!"

- "The triumph is being able to come out here under these kinds of conditions—and winning! As part of my mission, we conducted a spoiling attack against a motorized rifle company dug in—and we destroyed the entire company and still had two of the three teams left. And in the Valley of Death, conducting a defense, and although I had nothing left at the end of the battle, I had over seventy vehicles dead on and around my battle position. We stopped the entire regiment! I learned about time management and taking care of the soldiers. The soldiers will do what you tell them to do—but you've gotta take care of them. In my early missions I wasn't paying attention to the soldiers. In the later missions I paid attention to the soldiers and it made a difference. After one mission I pulled everybody in that we didn't need for security and gave them a little pep talk; the next day they killed everything that came toward us!"

- "As a staff officer out here, you have to pay attention to all the things that need to be done, so the company commander can pay attention to getting ready to fight the battle. As battalion S3, I was in charge of the TOC and didn't do everything I could to make sure the op order was ready on time, that the graphics were right, so that the company commander didn't have to call back in the middle of the night because he wasn't sure where he was. I learned a lot about time management and providing the services the commanders need to insure success."

- "Train the way you intend to fight! You have to train to a very high standard. That means everybody is there, they all have MILES and it works, you have an opposing force that is well equipped and is also ready to fight, that you don't have any distractions, that you employ as many of the combat multipliers as you possibly can. Then, when you go do it—and you screw it up—you come back and conduct a very honest and thorough AAR with a lot of candor with your subordinate leaders. You have to be willing to stand up and say, 'Guys, I screwed this up; I gave you a bad plan.' You make that assessment and go right back out and do it again, until you get it right!"

After twenty-one days or so, the troops pile back on the buses that will carry them to the planes and off to their units and families and homes. They've spent about two intense weeks in the closest thing to combat that peacetime will permit. Each soldier and each leader has lost something and won something. Each has been involved in losing battles and each has probably lost his life—at least once and perhaps many times—and by losing has gained some realistic

insights into the nature of his chosen profession and the risks and consequences of failure. Each has gained some realistic appreciation of the effectiveness of his unit and the unit's role in the greater plan of the parent units above. Each has also gained some sense of his unit's ability to react, learn, survive, and inflict damage on the enemy. Each soldier, leader, and commander comes away wiser in the ways of conflict in general and armored combat in particular. That means that each little element of the big fighting machine we call our Army is better prepared to do its business when and if it has to. When the business happens to be the defense of a nation's interests and institutions, that's a wonderful thing indeed.

The troops on the plane probably won't give much conscious thought to Mad Dog; they may

A T-72 flying the Jolly Roger heads in to the OPFOR motor pool after yet another successful war against the forces of imperialism.

not even know him by name or what he looks like. But they owe him and his tankers a salute. Those rough, tough soldiers of the 32d Guards Motorized Rifle Regiment are among the best friends American tankers could ask for. They've taught the advanced course in movement to contact, defense in sector, hasty and deliberate attack, plus all the rest. The visitors have been shown everything that can kill them, and have been brought back from the dead with the lessons fresh in their minds. War is the most serious business, with the possible exception of peace. Those who learn its lessons well can survive and prevail. And that's what the National Training Center is all about.

Inventory

WARSAW PACT EQUIPMENT AT NTC

BMP

The 32d Guards MRR tries to look like a typical first-rate Warsaw Pact outfit, and the vehicles it puts on the ground are a good mix of the best the Soviets and their comrades have available.

The most numerous at NTC, as elsewhere, is the BMP, which is simulated by a modified M551 Sheridan armored recon vehicle with fiberglass panels attached to make it look like the real thing. The BMP is a formidable beast on the battlefield. It isn't a tank, but an armored combat vehicle that comes in several flavors. The plain vanilla version has a low-profile turret and a 73mm gun. On the gun itself is mounted a launcher for the excellent Sagger antitank missile. It is a small, compact, fairly fast, well-armed fighting vehicle.

This combination of mobility, effective antitank firepower, and armor make the BMP highly dangerous to M1s and everything else the Blue force can oppose them with. The BMP main gun shoots a rocket-assisted, fin-stabilized projectile with a high-explosive charge that is effective out to 800 meters and has an automatic loader. The gun will kill medium tanks out to 1,300 meters, and for longer ranges the missile can be used to defeat targets out to 3,000 meters.

It is amphibious (not much of an asset at NTC) and can keep up with the fast movers on the ground, the T-72 tanks it usually supports in the assault.

The BMP carries eight additional weapons that are potentially the most dangerous on the battlefield—infantry. The vehicle commander is also a squad leader, and when the time comes, he and his troops dismount and go off in search of adventure. They don't have to get out to go to work, however, because the BMP has firing ports for each of them, and they can shoot their individual weapons from inside the beast when the occasion demands.

The BMP is a great concept and kills a lot of Americans at NTC, but it is not invulnerable. It didn't do too well against the Israelis in 1973, and there is an alleged debate within the Warsaw Pact military community about how to use it on the contemporary battlefield. Its armor is thin, and will not usually stop a .50-caliber armor-piercing (AP) projectile. The gun isn't stabilized, so it has to stop to shoot when moving across rough ground. The missile is difficult to reload. The gun can't be depressed much, which limits the usefulness of the beast in hull-down protected positions. Fuel and ammunition are vulnerable. Basically, the BMP has to come out in the open and hold still to shoot, and at close range if the gun is to be used. Neither of these are considered healthy tactical maneuvers. A lot of BMPs clutter up the battlefield at NTC, their kill lights flashing, after any sort of significant engagement. But they have usually helped buy victory. The latest version has a 30mm chain gun and an improved missile.

T-72

The basic tank of the Warsaw Pact nations currently is the T-72, a forty-one ton clanker

---

A Dragon antitank missile fires on a T-72. A small cartridge provides some of the flash and bang of the real missile.

A Soviet BMP is a sleek, dangerous, lightly armored vehicle that forms a large part of the Threat motor pool.

powered by a 700-horsepower engine, that the Soviets claim can go about sixty miles per hour. If there is anything the Soviets do well, it is designing tanks; this one is a winner. The engine is smooth running and smoke free, both important in the field. It will move the tank 500 klicks on a fill up (300 miles to those of you who haven't gone metric). With the two 100-gallon auxiliary tanks attached, it's good for 700 kilometers. It has good armor protection and includes skirt plates to protect the tracks. It has its own shovel mounted to the front of the hull, and can

dig itself in within a few minutes; the shovel also adds armor protection to the critical front portion of the hull. It is also set up to mount mine-clearing devices.

The T-72, like other modern Soviet tanks, has a turret that is elegant in design, a single, smooth casting in a kind of modified hemispheri-

cal form. It looks like it would let projectiles slide off with ease. The turret mounts a 125mm smooth-bore gun that shoots the latest thing in antiarmor projectiles, a fin-stabilized hypervelocity round that employs a discarding sabot. It seems to be the fastest gun in the west, or east, at a muzzle velocity of more than 1,615 meters per second and an effective range of at least 2,000 meters. This works out to about a mile a second, and that's quick. The Soviet gun concept is similar to the western concept—a flat trajectory and a short flight time, which permits little time for evasion and a good chance for a second shot. There's room aboard for forty rounds, with a usual mix of twelve hypervelocity armor-piercing fin-stabilized discarding sabots (HVAPFSDS), six high-explosive antitank (HEAT) rounds, and twenty-two high-explosive (HE) rounds. The gun has an automatic loader, which means that the crew need only be three men, which is just as well because it is a cramped turret.

The whole package is tidy and competent. It snorkels its way across rivers, protects its riders from air pollution, and generates smoke screens like a champ. Just to complicate things for the opposition, the Warsaw Pact guys have added reactive armor to this and many other of their armored vehicles. Reactive armor uses panels of explosives that go off when struck by the blast from a shaped-charge weapon like a TOW missile. This reactive armor produced quite a reaction among western military planners when it was revealed that the TOW missiles and all

Real Soviet armor, like these somewhat obsolete T-62s, shows a practical and elegant flair for design not apparent in the VISMOD imitations. That turret looks like it could shed a direct hit by a nuclear device.

the other shaped-charge weapons might be suddenly obsolete. It has turned out to be less of a
problem than originally thought, but it shows
that the real OPFOR is innovative and imagina-
tive, and unwilling to maintain the status quo.

ZSU

The ZSU-23-4 helps provide air defense for
an MRR. It is a four-barreled 23mm automatic
antiaircraft gun on a modified light tank chassis.
It has its own radar fire-control system. It can
acquire and track high- and low-flying aircraft
and engage them effectively within 3,000 meters.
It is also useful against ground targets like light
armor and infantry.

An M1A1 rumbles off on its mission. The highly capable
M1 is the foundation for U.S. defense strategy, using technological quality against numerical superiority.

AMERICAN TANKS AND FIGHTING VEHICLES

M1A1/M1

The M1 is considered by those who own and
operate it the best main battle tank in the world,
but that's hard to determine without a shoot-off.
It is neither the biggest nor the most expensive,
those honors going to German, British, and Israeli

models. There is a possibility that the Soviets' new T-80 is more expensive, but they aren't telling.

It has a 1,500-horsepower gas turbine engine that will take it from zero to 20 miles per hour in six seconds, and that's not bad for a sporty model that weighs 60 tons. It will cruise along at better than 45 miles per hour on favorable ground. This speed and dash capability is part of the tank's offensive punch and defensive armor. There are 275 gallons of fuel aboard, and you get about 1.5 miles to the gallon (freeway), or about 1.0 (city).

The M1 was the first American tank to incorporate some developments that have been part of tank design in Britain and elsewhere over the last couple of decades, the new armor being the first and foremost.

It uses the latest thing in armor—an advanced variety of the concept developed in Britain in the 1960s—a series of layers of metals and materials that deflect and dissipate the effect of both

The M1 Abrams in the A1 version. The turret has what's called a ''needle-nosed'' design with angular sides, the better to shed the angry fates and sad misfortunes of war.

shaped-charge weapons (like TOW missiles) and kinetic energy weapons (like hypervelocity penetrators). While it was being tested, more than 3,500 antiarmor rounds were fired at fully loaded tanks, which were still able to drive away. A system for fire suppression inside the vehicle uses Halon gas and a quick reaction suppression system to extinguish any flames that get going inside.

The cost of the M1 was an issue a few years ago when it was getting into production, and the figure of $2.7 million was frequently cited. That figure includes all the changes and all the spare parts and related programs involved in the whole contract. In fact, you can buy fifteen to twenty M1s for what you'd have to pay for a single fighter aircraft.

The M1 series carries twice the ammo load for the machine guns that the M60 series stows. There is room for fifty-five rounds of 105mm ammunition on the M1, and for about forty rounds for the 120mm gun on the M1A1.

M60A3

The M60 is the previous top-of-the-line main battle tank, pride of the Army from 1959 until about 1980, when the newer M1 took over. It puts forty-eight tons of fighting steel on the ground, will zip around at about thirty miles per hour, and on a good day will rumble across three hundred miles of reasonable roadway. Its gun was the latest thing when it was developed by the British, a 105mm high-velocity design

M60A3 tank. Slower, noisier, but with very similar weapons and sights, the M60 is a capable performer. Its 120mm main gun is the same as the M1's—here sending a sabot round off to kill a target two kilometers away.

that will pump out sixty-three rounds of APDS, HEAT, and other types of ammunition before the cupboard goes bare on the loader. It has .50-caliber and 7.62mm machine guns. It is powered by one of those weird engines that tank designers always seem to come up with—an air-cooled V12 diesel that produces 750 horsepower, at least on paper.

The upgraded version is the A3, and it has a 900-horsepower engine, thermal sights, laser range finder, and a stabilization system for the big gun. It is a pretty capable package, and suffers only by comparison to the M1.

M2 AND M3 BRADLEY ARMORED FIGHTING VEHICLES

The Bradley is something of a new idea for the United States Army, which has taken the lead from the Soviets and others in the armor design community. Although the M2 is often confused with the old M113 APC, there is a radical difference in philosophy about how the two machines are supposed to work and fight and survive on the battlefield. The philosophy starts with the name; the Bradley is a fighting vehicle, the M113 is a personnel carrier. In fact, the Bradley is a BMP killer, which is interesting, because it is based a lot on the BMP itself. Both are designed to complement the big guns of the tanks with smaller guns for lighter targets. There is a lot of light armor on the battlefield, and that light armor carries all sorts of heavy weapons like TOW missiles and similar firepower.

The Bradley comes in two variants. The first carries troops, the chain gun, and TOW missiles, all three of which are potent killers. The M3 cavalry fighting vehicle is a different breed of cat; it is a scout that ranges far and wide on

A Bradley from the 2d Armored Division at Fort Hood. The Bradley is as fast as the M1, eats BMPs for breakfast, and is admired by its crews.

behalf of the commander, snooping, shooting, and scooting. It is tasked particularly with making the call for fire, bringing down the wrath of the fire-support officer.

The Bradley has taken a lot of criticism from the press in its early years, much to the dismay of the troopers who use it. It certainly costs more than the M113 APC and carries (in the M3 version) fewer troops. But the M2 was intended to be a completely different animal. It is faster, and can keep up with the M1, which the 113 was unable to do; it is much more resistant to artillery and other hazards than the APC. It has had a few teething problems, but all new systems do. The essential difference between it and the old, cheap, slow, vulnerable APC is that the Bradley has a killing role on the battlefield; it is a BMP killer of the best kind. When it works

as a team with the M1 tank, the Soviet armor formations have something to worry about. When the Bradley started showing up at NTC, the results were noticeable immediately in the flashing kill lights of the light armor. The OPFOR is candidly afraid of the M2s and M3s, and is having trouble dealing with the Bradley; it is eating their light armor for lunch. This means the M1s and M60s can deal with the T-72s and not have to worry about the little guys so much. This is an exciting development if you want to discourage the Red Horde from crossing the European fence.

M113 ARMORED PERSONNEL CARRIER

If you judge by numbers, the armored personnel carrier is the most popular track on the battlefield. The Soviets and the NATO allies use them by the tens of thousands. And the M113 is the hands-down champion of the western powers, with more than 60,000 in circulation around the world. It has more modifications and variants than you'd see at a hot-rod show. The M113 comes to work in all sorts of costumes; people add things to it for just about every mission short of flight that you can imagine. It has had all sorts of weapons on it, including cannon, lots of different kinds of rockets, machine guns, and flamethrowers. Instead of troops, some carry mortars, radios, commanders, or just groceries and expendables.

In the battlefield tour-bus configuration—the basic APC—the beast carries thirteen troops—a crew of two and a cast of eleven infantry who get off at the first stop. It weighs about eleven tons, and is powered by a V8 diesel engine that will push it along at about forty miles per hour under the best of circumstances. It will cover about three hundred miles before you need to pull it into a service station.

It is called an armored personnel carrier, but the stuff they call armor is not what you want between you and any respectable antiarmor weapon. The APC is built of welded aluminum plate, and in Viet Nam, rocket-propelled grenades worked quite well against them. The M113 was really designed just to protect troops against the kind of hazards of battlefields of the Korean War vintage, small arms fire, and artillery fragments. It does pretty well at deflecting both of those, but there are now so many light antitank weapons (LAWs) west of the Pecos that the vehicle is not as popular as it was in its youth. Just the same, there are a lot of them out there, and they're working hard, at NTC and around the world.

M109 SELF-PROPELLED HOWITZER

All artillery is portable, but some more so than others. The 109 is a big gun on a big set of tracks, and it goes in harm's way with its accomplices—the tanks and the infantry. It is the most popular self-propelled howitzer in the world. A howitzer, by the way, is a medium-to-low-velocity artillery piece that uses an arcing trajectory to tactical advantage. It looks like the meanest gun on the battlefield, but it is not the thickest skinned track around. The armor is less than an inch thick at best, and that means an antitank weapon could take it out.

The gun is 155mm and fires all sorts of packages to more than 18,000 meters, about 10 miles. Ammunition includes HE (high explosive), smoke, illumination rounds, chemical, and tactical nuclear. But one of the most useful projectiles carries lots of little land mines. The mines are field artillery scatterable mines (FASCAM) and will blow the track off a tank. If you fire a FASCAM barrage in front of or over an attacking armor force, they've got to come to a screeching halt or find a way of dealing with your fresh mine field.

Six troops operate a 109. It takes a strong trooper to hump the projectile, which weighs about sixty pounds. The 109 will achieve thirty-five miles per hour on a good day with a tail wind. There are well over 4,000 of them and they are serving in armies around the world, sometimes shooting at each other.

ANTIARMOR WEAPONS

TOW

The tube-launched, optically tracked, wire command link guided missile (TOW) is considered a heavy antiarmor weapon. It is heavy in several respects—it weighs 226 pounds complete and will not fit in your rucksack. The missile will, however, fly slowly out to about three and a half kilometers (two miles or so) and do a lot of damage when it arrives. Its warhead will cut through a foot and a half of steel, four feet of concrete, or eight feet of earth and ruin the day for anybody on the other side. The figures for concrete and soil are important because, besides killing tanks, bunkers are one of its appropriate targets. The TOW takes four guys to make it work. It usually rides around on a variation of the M113 called an improved TOW vehicle, or on the wonderful all-terrain utility vehicle nicknamed the Hummer. The latest version of the TOW comes with an improved night sight and guidance system.

That's a VISMOD T-72 out there, acting cooperative for the camera and for the Dragon team out in the open. In real life it's a good idea to hide first, shoot second.

DRAGON

The fire-breathing Dragon, like the TOW, is a wire-guided missile that was intended to defeat the biggest and baddest armor anybody had. And it could, too, in 1965. The Dragon is good to a thousand meters (six-tenths of a mile), when it works. It will go through a foot of steel, four feet of concrete, or eight feet of soil. The M47 Dragon is only a thirty-two-pound package, which means one poor guy can hump it across the battlefield. It has a thermal sight, which you keep after you shoot the round. You toss away the old tube and attach the sight to a fresh missile tube.

The Dragon is not the most reliable weapon. It was designed and most were built a decade or two back, and the electronics and related goodies are not what they used to be. A fair number of missiles, when fired, leave the tube and go flopping downrange in a dramatic but ineffective display of fireworks. A Dragon is not the easiest thing to shoot either: When it fires, it moves forward, the center of gravity suddenly shifts, and the gunner tends to be looking at the ground. If you don't recover fast and accurately, you will have just wasted about $2,200 worth of fireworks.

Both the Dragon and the TOW have some problems for the contemporary army, problems on the minds of people who come to NTC. The missiles are slow, which means you've got to track the target for perhaps ten or twelve seconds. This may not sound like much, but it is an eternity when a drenching artillery barrage is falling around you. Firing a Dragon or a TOW are both guaranteed to make everybody on the opposing team notice you right away, and they will all take a sincere and immediate interest in you. Even if you have the steely disposition to hang in there and track the target, all the little chunks of slightly used artillery shells flying through space can cut the tiny wires between you and the missile, and the thing will flop around on the ground.

But both weapons have their times and places, and both will do some killing. The TOW is being slung on lots of vehicles and helicopters, all of which become somewhat vulnerable when they go to work. But nobody is safe on the battlefield. New systems are being designed and tested, and no doubt an improved missile will come along to displace these.

LAW

The light antitank weapon (LAW) was con-ceived as a last-ditch, close-in, shaped-charge weapon that had a chance of killing armor, and could also be used for bunker busting. That was a long time ago, when tanks had thinner armor made of simple steel. Tanks have since stopped cooperating with the intentions of the designers of the LAW by using much thicker and much more effective material to protect themselves. The LAW is still a good weapon to have around, though, because it is effective against the lighter armor of a BMP, BTR, or BRDM. And it is useful on those occasions when the loyal opposition has gone to ground and some concrete, logs, or soil stand between you and them.

The LAW is light and compact; the little rocket is only 66mm in diameter. If you can hit anything with the LAW at two hundred meters, they'll pin a sharpshooter medal on your shirt; beyond that, it's strictly luck. But if it does hit steel, it will go through eight inches worth; it's good for two feet of concrete and six feet of dirt. Or so the Army hopes.

The LAW is a round of ammunition rather than a weapon in the conventional sense, and when you've had your way with it, you just discard its empty launch tube. There are a zillion LAWs stacked away in bunkers, awaiting the call, and just about every trooper will have one or two.

AT4M136

The LAW is being replaced by an improved version—an 84mm recoilless rifle round (not a rocket) that is fin stabilized and is good out to almost 300 meters. It will still not be 100 percent effective against Soviet tanks, but it will probably do better than the LAW against lightweight armor.

About the Author/Photographer

Hans Halberstadt is a writer, photographer, and corporate film producer who sometimes lives in San Jose, California, when he is recovering from trips to Fort Irwin. Halberstadt spent three years in the U.S. Army, which included a year in Viet Nam where he was a helicopter gunner. That experience resulted in an abiding interest in life and death issues which influences most of his projects. Previous books include USCG: ALWAYS READY, AIRBORNE: ASSAULT FROM THE SKY, GREEN BERETS: UNCONVENTIONAL WARRIORS, and STAINED GLASS: MUSIC FOR THE EYE.